Praise for *Taking*

I adore the honesty of this straight-talking book: it allows you to see the sunshine through the trees when it comes to school inspections.

Paul takes you every step of the way in *Taking Control 2*, from the pre-inspection phone call to getting your self-evaluation form in order. The appendices on self-evaluations are very useful, and the real-life examples from real schools really adds meat onto the bones of the book. Furthermore, the highlighted page references to the framework are simply perfect and make cross-referencing an effortless task for the reader.

A treasure chest of support and guidance.

Chris Dyson, Head Teacher, Parklands Primary School

Authentic, considered and practical, *Taking Control 2* provides a welcome pathway to help educators navigate both the nuisance and the challenge created by the 2019 education inspection framework (EIF). The knowledge and experience that Paul shares, combined with his evidence-based interrogation of the framework, equips school leaders with a blueprint for success. Moreover, the book is littered with realistic and ethical humanity – something our profession needs now more than ever.

Nicole Fowles, Head Teacher and Lead Learner, Coleshill Heath School

Taking Control 2 is both highly informative and very instructive, and is especially helpful considering we have an imminent inspection at one of our schools. I have been previously involved in two inspections under the previous framework, and this book clearly points out the emphasis change in the new EIF.

David Valentine, Chair of Trustees, Barnsole Primary Trust

Once again, Paul Garvey has provided clear guidance on how to prepare for an Ofsted inspection. In addition, he provides thought-provoking discussion and challenge regarding school improvement and the role Ofsted plays within this. *Taking Control 2* is a great read and an invaluable toolkit.

Jim Garbutt, executive head teacher

'Forewarned is forearmed,' writes Paul Garvey in the introduction to *Taking Control 2*, and that's the key message of the book. Speaking with authority and insight, he walks school leaders through the Ofsted inspection journey, giving clear guidance and useful tips along the way. As he makes clear, this isn't a guide on how to pull the wool over inspectors' eyes and neither is it a substitute for effective school improvement – it's a step-by-step, eminently readable manual that shows how to understand the process and make sure the strengths of your school are highlighted and celebrated. The nuances of the 2019 EIF are clearly presented and the book has the ring of authenticity throughout.

Garvey has a well-deserved reputation as someone who fights the corner of schools and school leaders, and this book is written from that perspective. I highly recommend it.

Dr Paul Heery, CEO, White Hills Park Trust

PAUL GARVEY

TAKING 2
CONTROL

HOW TO PREPARE FOR OFSTED UNDER THE EDUCATION INSPECTION FRAMEWORK

Crown House Publishing Limited
www.crownhouse.co.uk

First published by

Crown House Publishing Ltd
Crown Buildings, Bancyfelin, Carmarthen, Wales, SA33 5ND, UK
www.crownhouse.co.uk

and

Crown House Publishing Company LLC
PO Box 2223, Williston, VT 05495, USA
www.crownhousepublishing.com

First published 2020. Reprinted 2021.

Quotes from Ofsted and Department for Education documents used in this
publication have been approved under an Open Government Licence. Please see:
http://www.nationalarchives.gov.uk/doc/open-government-licence/version/3/.

Crown House Publishing has no responsibility for the persistence or accuracy of
URLs for external or third-party websites referred to in this publication, and does not
guarantee that any content on such websites is, or will remain, accurate or appropriate.

British Library Cataloguing-in-Publication Data

A catalogue entry for this book is available
from the British Library.

Print ISBN 978-178583487-5
Mobi ISBN 978-178583494-3
ePub ISBN 978-178583495-0
ePDF ISBN 978-178583496-7

LCCN 2020931176

Printed and bound in the UK by
Charlesworth Press, Wakefield, West Yorkshire

This book is dedicated to my Twitter professional learning network (OK, followers, but I hate that word!). Without their encouragement (OK, nagging!) this book would still be in my head, waiting to be written. My Twitter PLN is, quite simply, wonderful. Thank you.

PROLOGUE

Thank you so much for buying *Taking Control 2*!

This book's predecessor, *Taking Control*, helped many schools to prepare for inspection under the previous Ofsted inspection framework. We now have a greatly changed framework, the 2019 education inspection framework, ostensibly based largely on the inspection of a school's curriculum. Ofsted call curriculum the 'substance' of education. These changes to inspection are bigger than those I have seen in any update, of any framework, I have known – and I inspected schools for 11 years. This new inspection focus – and the new methodology that Ofsted are employing – is causing problems for schools. Schools need help; hence this book. There is huge concern about increased workload in preparation for 'deep dives', especially from leaders of foundation subjects and those in primary schools. The expectations for classroom teachers, of whom I could say 'do nothing extra' before September 2019, are also raised in this framework. To a lesser extent, they need to be ready for inspection too.

This book will help at all levels and in all types of maintained schools. It will alleviate some of those worries, stop schools piling unnecessary work onto staff and help leaders to feel much more confident about facing inspection. This book looks at inspection from an inspector's point of view, includes a wealth of experiences from schools of actual inspections under the 2019 framework and also contains dialogic tools for writing your self-evaluation form, whether for a primary or a secondary school.

CONTENTS

INTRODUCTION

The education inspection framework introduced in September 2019 is a very different beast from all the previous Ofsted frameworks. If you have bought this book, you are likely to be in a school that will soon be on the opposite end of a 90-minute phone call from someone like me.

If so, read *Taking Control 2* with the relevant Ofsted handbook at your side or, even better and far more green, on screen. There are many references to paragraphs and pages (always in grey) in the section 5 (S5) and section 8 (S8) handbooks or the framework (EIF) where you can investigate the detail further, should you need to do so.

This book, like its predecessor,[1] gives you the inside story on inspection. The Latin saying *praemonitus, praemunitus* loosely translates as 'forewarned is forearmed' – and with inspections being so enormously high stakes today, schools really do need to be forewarned and you really do need to be metaphorically armed to the proverbial teeth in readiness for your inspectors. Be under no illusion: inspection is a battle that can definitely be won or lost.

Ofsted suggest you shouldn't do anything extra to your day-to-day activities to prepare for inspection, and I – and every single one of the schools I have supported through their inspections and many others – say that's mad!

Ofsted won't allow their independent inspectors to offer advice to schools; thus, Ofsted wouldn't allow me to both inspect and to write a book like this. I said 'someone like me' above. Some time ago, Ofsted's intransigence on inspectors helping schools caused me to stop inspecting. I loved helping schools, and still do, but hanging up my inspector's badge allowed me to write *Taking Control* and this, its sequel.

Ofsted have a large team of just over 1,500 inspectors whose main remit is to inspect in the education, learning and skills sector. They inspect mainstream schools and academies; over 70% of these inspectors are

---

1   Paul Garvey, *Taking Control: How to Prepare for Inspection* (Woodbridge: John Catt, 2017).

serving professionals in schools. They have another 320 who inspect mainly in early years and a handful who inspect mainly in the social care sector.[2]

There is an annual churn of inspectors. Over 200 joined in the period June 2018 to June 2019 and well over 400 left in the same 12-month period. As a result, your inspection team may lack experience, so it is worth asking your lead inspector what depth of inspection experience they and their team possess. It will also take some time until inspectors are experienced with the EIF. Almost all will be 'feeling their way' (as one school put it) in their early days.

All these inspectors could be licensed to support schools in inspection preparation, but the organisation chooses instead to prevent this excellent workforce from doing so. Of course, Ofsted inspectors do help, and of those I know, both those serving in schools and those who are independent Ofsted inspectors, all use their knowledge in some way to help schools or as part of their work in schools or multi-academy trusts (MATs). Ofsted's stance means this advice has to be given below the organisation's radar. That is not me. I am just too open and honest about supporting schools to prepare for inspection. This book could not have been written by any of Ofsted's inspectors who wish to continue to inspect, but it is a book that I hope many schools will find extremely useful.

Although Ofsted maintain that schools should not prepare for inspection, your inspectors will be making mental notes about how effective leaders and managers are throughout your inspection. They will be thinking, 'Has this leadership team got the "capacity for improving the quality of education provided by the school"?' (p. 75, S5, in the bullet list for 'inadequate'). If it becomes clear that leaders at all levels don't know the school as well as your inspectors might like you to – and especially if there is seen to be no coherent plan for progression in the school's curriculum – it will cause you problems and overhang your inspection. If your inspectors feel that leaders are not well briefed and organised, this question may well raise its head, if not for an inadequate grade then as a counterweight to good. It will supplement thinking around other

---

2   A list of current inspectors and their remits can be found at: https://www.gov.uk/government/publications/ofsted-inspectors-list.

reasons why leadership and management may not be judged as positively as you would like it to be. It is the first 'unknown unknown' for which you may need to be prepared (see page 14).

In the previous framework, it was senior leaders who needed to be prepared. In this EIF, it is subject leaders and even classroom teachers who must be ready to face some detailed questioning about curriculum organisation. This includes subject leaders in small primary schools who may be leading subjects with no financial reward and in their first years of teaching. It also includes all teachers of all subjects. Ofsted's expectation is that every teacher should be able to talk about the curriculum in their subject. The handbook (para. 189, p. 46, S5; my emphasis) makes this abundantly clear:

The following activities will provide inspectors with evidence about the school's implementation of its intended curriculum:

▪ discussions with curriculum and subject leaders *and teachers* about the programme of study that classes are following for particular subjects or topics, the intended end points towards which those pupils are working, and their view of how those pupils are progressing through the curriculum.

Ofsted also expect subject leaders to be able to talk about their subject with confidence, with reference to starting points and end points, in all years in the school, including the early years and sixth form. It is a big ask of middle leaders, especially in primary schools, and is an unfairness of this framework.

This book will help teachers, together with subject leaders and their line managers in senior leadership, to prepare for inspection. It will give you the knowledge to face those inspection meetings and activities with confidence.

In the previous framework, classroom teachers and assistants had next to no need for preparation. This time, observations – with subject leaders, not senior leaders – are back on the agenda. No grades will be given by inspectors, but a knowledge of where the lesson sits in the school's subject curriculum now has a much higher profile. In *Taking Control* I was able to say that 'Any extra inspection preparation pressure put on classroom teachers and their assistants by leaders – or by themselves, as teachers can be their own worst enemy sometimes – is unnecessary.'[3] I can't do that now. It is well worth classroom teachers demonstrating that their pupils know what they have learned and what they are about to learn. Inspectors will ask them. In addition, my previous advice to classroom teachers and assistants still stands: speak positively with inspectors and follow your school's policies, especially around behaviour.

It is good to see that Ofsted have removed teaching from any of the main judgement categories, but this does not mean they won't look at teaching on inspection. If anything, the EIF increases the use of what they see in lessons. Ofsted's main expectations of teachers can be found in the section 5 handbook (para. 183, p. 44).

I go further than believing that teachers, subject leaders and senior leaders, including governors, should prepare for inspection. I firmly believe that leaders can *take control* of the process. What this book will do is give you the best chance possible of inspection success.

This book also gives your school the best chance possible to get the inspection grade you believe you deserve. It will enable you to construct compelling arguments that your Ofsted inspector will find difficult to counter. A feature of this book is a concentration on schools' knowledge of curriculum progression, but data (or information) is still important, especially when assessing the impact of the school's work. Published data will give your lead inspector their initial feel for your school. If, at face value, these data do not look positive, that must be countered and explained, in a persuasive self-evaluation form (SEF).

Although Ofsted would like you to feel that curriculum is now the main focus of inspection, it will be interesting to see how many schools with poorer data are judged to be good or outstanding. I predict few, and probably similar percentages to the previous framework. Curriculum may now be Ofsted's king, but data is now the joker in the pack that could upset your outcome.

---

3   Paul Garvey, *Taking Control*, p. 7.

This book is for you …

- If you know that you are leading a good (grade 2) school, but your inspection data summary report (IDSR) may be suggesting otherwise.

- If you are leading a good school but you have made improvements from your last inspection, and believe that you may now be an outstanding school, and want your inspectors to recognise this.

- If you believe you are leading an outstanding school, ostensibly exempt from inspection, doing amazing things, but are worried that this framework may preclude another grade 1.

- If you are leading a school that is grade 3 or grade 4 and you are improving from difficult times, but you need Ofsted to listen to what is now possible in the future.

- If you are a subject leader or classroom teacher and you are worried by the raised expectations on you, inherent in this new inspection regime.

- If you are a governor or trustee who needs to understand the inspection process, as you will be interviewed by the inspection team, and you want to support your head teacher/principal to the fullest.

An important piece of knowledge for all schools is that the interpretation of every single criterion in the inspection handbook is subjective. It is down to the interpretation of your inspectors. That is where this book can help.

My advice is to be forearmed because, if your preparation is lacking, the handbook may well give your inspectors licence to find reasons to say you are not as good as you feel and know you are. The grade given to a school has to add up. Things have to satisfy a 'best fit' of subjective judgements around the criteria for four grades and your grade for overall effectiveness.

Grade 1 – outstanding.

Grade 2 – good.

Grade 3 – requires improvement.

Grade 4 – inadequate.

The quality assurance process at Ofsted doesn't give either Ofsted inspectors or Her Majesty's Inspectors (HMI) the freedom to report that a school is good if the handbook criteria are not satisfied well enough, and all HMI and lead inspectors know this. But it is possible for you to help them towards their decision through what you do before and during your inspection.

With the help of this book, you can be subtle and clever enough to help your lead inspector to write the inspection report you would like to read. Inspectors are very well trained in the use of the handbook, but, to be blunt, *you* have to know the inspection handbook as well as, if not better than, your inspectors. Know it well enough to be able to quote from it to back up your position.

I will refer to what are currently the most recent versions of the handbook, but please check at www.gov.uk for the most up-to-date editions:

> The current section 5 handbook can be found at: https://www.gov.uk/government/publications/school-inspection-handbook-eif.

> The current section 8 handbook can be found at: https://www.gov.uk/government/publications/section-8-school-inspection-handbook-eif.

> The current education inspection framework (which includes Ofsted's methodology on deep dives) can be found at: https://www.gov.uk/government/publications/education-inspection-framework.

The handbooks are extremely detailed and rather arcane documents, but schools must be cognisant with their intricacies. If not, you will be faced with a lead inspector who is very familiar with the handbooks, which can leave you vulnerable. I will help you throughout with clear references to the parts that I think are most helpful to schools.

Types of inspections

In state schools, inspections come in two forms: section 5 and section 8 inspections. In 2005, these replaced earlier section 10 inspections from the relevant section of the Schools Inspections Act 1996, in which they were established in law. More experienced (OK, older!) readers may remember those big teams descending on your school and looking at every subject, after you had spent the six-week(!) lead-in time working yourselves silly to prepare.

Section 5 inspections last two days and grades are given. They usually occur when a previously requires improvement or inadequate school undergoes its next inspection. In addition, if a good school undergoes a section 8 inspection and inspectors feel there is evidence that the school has improved towards outstanding or may no longer be good, inspectors will specify that the next inspection is a section 5 inspection, with the full range of graded judgements available (para. 29, p. 10, S5). They can also occur when a school requests an inspection (para. 31, p. 10, S5).

Section 8 inspections almost always last two days, but in schools with fewer than 150 pupils it will be just one day. It results in a letter, but no grades are given; a section 8 inspection cannot change the overall effectiveness grade for the school. These usually occur when a previously good school undergoes its next inspection, which takes place every four years. They also occur if previously outstanding schools, exempt from inspection, are identified as having declined in performance, via Ofsted's annual monitoring. There are other possible reasons for a section 8 inspection which are set out in the relevant handbooks. In exceptional circumstances, section 8 inspections can be 'converted' to section 5 inspections and extra team members brought in. This will then result in grades being given.

Section 8 inspections actually give the inspectorate the power to perform inspections at any time and for any reason, at the discretion of Her Majesty's Chief Inspector of Schools (HMCI). These inspections are known as section 8 inspections with 'no formal designation'. Basically, Ofsted can look at anything in their remit, any time they wish. Fortunately, these are fairly rare and come about due to specific reasons, as laid out in the handbook (paras 218–224, p. 49, S8). These apply especially to exempt schools and are a way for Ofsted to inspect a previously outstanding school if:

- There are any safeguarding concerns, including a decline in the standards of pupils' behaviour and the ability of staff to maintain discipline, and/or welfare concerns.

- A subject or thematic survey inspection raises more general concerns.

- A qualifying complaint is received which, taken alongside other available evidence, suggests they should inspect the school.

- Concerns are raised about standards of leadership or governance.

- Concerns are identified about the curriculum (including if the statutory requirement to publish information to parents is not met).

- HMCI or the secretary of state have concerns about a school's performance.

That is, just about anything!

In 2012, section 8 'short inspections' of previously good mainstream schools were introduced, but these have now gone in the EIF. All good schools now receive two-day inspections every (approximately) four years, as do outstanding (and good) nurseries, pupil referral units and special schools.

Complicated? Yes. Overcomplicated? Very probably, but Ofsted are subject to legislation and can't change the inspection parameters. It is worth referring to the handbooks for precise and up-to-date information on the type of inspection you may face and the timings. Ofsted changed these during the previous framework and may well change them during this framework too.

Following a section 5 inspection, schools are given a judgement of overall effectiveness. Schools receiving a grade 4 and a proportion of those receiving a grade 3 receive further section 8 monitoring inspections until they are graded good, although conversion to academy status now complicates inspection timings. If a school is graded inadequate and placed in 'special measures', it is likely to face forced academisation and be required to join a MAT, not of its choosing.

A lead inspector of both section 5 and section 8 inspections can be either an HMI (salaried to Ofsted) or an Ofsted inspector who is independent of Ofsted, working on an ad hoc basis and performing a number of inspections each year. These inspectors can be serving professionals in schools.

A chink of light has recently been provided. Ofsted had to change the grade at a West London Academy following a complaint.[4] This is the first change for six years.

It is a complex situation, generally well known to senior leaders in schools, but sometimes difficult for other staff in schools to appreciate the full details. For an explanation of why we have this split between section 5 inspections of requires improvement and inadequate schools, section 8 inspections of good schools, and the fact that outstanding schools are exempt from regular inspection, see section 1.3.

Taking Control 2 will aid those leaders of good schools in persuading their Ofsted inspector/HMI that they do not need to alert Ofsted in their section 8 inspection letter to reinspect because standards have fallen. It will also aid such leaders if they feel that the section 8 inspection of their currently good school really does need to look, quickly, at whether it is now an outstanding school.

Ofsted no longer presume that a previously good school is still good, but after reviewing your data, pre-inspection, all HMI/Ofsted inspectors will have formed initial ideas about the school that they will need to test out. However, hopefully they will not have made any judgements. Long experience of inspecting has taught me that you never know what you will find when you walk through the doors of a school, but not all inspectors are the same. If you get the feeling that your lead inspector is trying to fit what they are seeing to a preconceived idea of what the school must be like, based on its outcomes, ask the lead inspector to leave your office and call the Ofsted helpline on 0300 123 1231 immediately and ask to speak to the duty HMI.

---

4 Helene Mulholland, Ofsted amends 'inadequate' grade after curriculum inspection complaints, *Schools Week* (31 January 2019). Available at: https://schoolsweek. co.uk/ofsted-amends-inadequate-grade-after-curriculum-inspection-complaints/ amp/?__twitter_impression=true.

Please don't leave this to a later complaint. After supporting many schools through complaints and listening to the experiences of many head teachers and principals, I have come to the opinion that the Ofsted complaints procedure is so stacked against complaining schools, and in favour of the inspectorate, that it is not worth the paper on which it is written. A recent Freedom of Information (FOI) request found that not a single inspection grade had changed as a result of a complaint in the period 2014–2019. I find that quite incredible, in the true sense of the word. It is unbelievable. Ofsted can't have got every single inspection right over this five-year period, but that is effectively what they are suggesting with the zero changes in grades via complaints. Good luck if you ever have to cope with this badly flawed procedure.

Always remember that all grades and criteria are subjective. Your lead inspector has to evidence any decisions they make to get their eventual section 8 letter or final section 5 report through quality assurance. This gives you the lever to influence and persuade. It is possible to take control of your inspection. It really is!

A very persuasive SEF (the acronym means self-evaluation form, although there is now no compulsory form to fill in, as there was at the start of section 5 inspections in 2005 – it is just a self-evaluation of your school, but SEF survives in common parlance, so I will use it as an abbreviation throughout) combined with a confident demeanour from all leaders on inspection is needed. Marry this with clear and accurate references to improvements and link this in your SEF to relevant sections in the inspection handbook. This can plant the seed of an idea that your school is at least good and may be better, if that is what you are aiming for.

In addition, if they don't see you confidently helping them towards their decision, even though their pre-inspection view of the school is positive, your inspectors will be making unspoken value judgements about whether leadership and management are really driving improvements towards a good or an outstanding school, or whether they still have some way to go. *Take control.* Provide your lead inspector with all the information they need in order to make the decisions you want them to make, and deliver all the necessary information with confidence, belief and persuasiveness. Taking control will also help if you are a grade 2 school undergoing your four-yearly section 8 inspection, and you really don't want that inspection to result in a letter saying Ofsted will come back earlier to look at requires improvement.

Ostensibly, section 8 inspections don't result in grades. In reality, of course, the inspectors are always thinking grades. You should know how your lead inspector is thinking, as they are tasked to keep you up to date with how the inspection is going. This is especially true at the end of an inspection. The inspector will tell you then why they are not convinced you are still a grade 2 school. This is obviously an outcome you want to avoid, if possible. It will lead to a section 5 inspection within two years, and that team will have the letter you received following your section 8 inspection firmly in mind. This two-year period can be stressful, but it can also be used to effect the improvements the lead inspector's letter asks of you. All hope is by no means lost, but this time make sure you take control of that section 5 inspection. However, if schools like these could have been more convincing on their section 8 inspection days, they may not have had to endure a full section 5 inspection. If this is why you are reading this book, *Taking Control 2* will give you those tools of persuasion.

The possibility of a grade slip is perhaps the most difficult inspection situation. If it is a catastrophic slip to inadequate, as all presently good or requires improvement schools know, this opens up the potential abyss of forced conversion to an academy, and perhaps being swallowed up and 'sponsored' by an academy chain which, if you had a choice, you would not consider joining. The option of determining your own future in an academy-dominated educational world may be taken away from you, simply because of an inspection decision which may have been brought about through not knowing what you could have done to prepare fully. This can happen all too easily if you fail to show an inspection team that you are actually a good or requires improvement school that has turned a corner, and the future is actually a lot brighter than your current IDSR suggests. This book will give you the best possible chance of persuading your lead inspector/HMI that this is the case. The stakes are abominably high.

On the other side of the fence, so to speak, academy chains and MATs are under scrutiny from a government which expects results in terms of school improvement. The main and very crude measure that is being used to judge MAT success is changes in Ofsted grades of the schools that comprise the MAT or chain. As the MAT will have been expected to assimilate a potentially significant number of grade 3 and grade 4 schools, it is extremely important that the strongest possible arguments are offered to demonstrate the improvement of individual schools to inspection teams. An improving set of Ofsted grades over time, or maintenance of existing good grades, is a very strong argument for Ofsted, in discussion with the regional schools commissioner, to not perform a full and potentially damaging inspection of the MAT or academy chain. This book is also for those MATs.

What this book can't do is save you

If your school does not give pupils a leg-up in their life chances, from joining your school to leaving, there is nothing this book can do to help you change your likely Ofsted grade. If pupil progress from their starting points is poor – and I will detail many ways in which you can show good progress from starting points – or leadership and management is poor, or behaviour is not under control, something in your school has to change. If safeguarding is not right, I have no sympathy. You must get it right. If your pupils are not getting a good deal over time, please don't look to the contents of this book as your safe passage. If you are in that position, I would have had no hesitation in giving you a grade 4, and I would expect your inspectors to do exactly the same.

I believe that schools need to be held to account if they are not performing well. I support a supportive, professional monitoring process, and although I agree with Ofsted on some things, I no longer feel that they are competent enough to be responsible for inspection. Too much hubris, too many Department for Education agendas, too many flaws.

However, if it is simply that you are finding it hard to *demonstrate* that the pupils in your school are getting a good deal over time, but actually staff, leaders, parents and pupils feel that they are, then *Taking Control 2* is definitely for you.

There is a moral base to the school inspection process to which I, and almost every inspector I have ever met, subscribe. I inspected for the pupils; not for head teachers or principals, not for senior leaders, not for teachers or teaching assistants, not for governors or MAT boards. There was only one reason I inspected (and it certainly wasn't for the money, which really does not recompense lead inspectors for the responsibility of leading inspections, which is huge), and that was to ensure that the pupils in a school were getting the best deal possible for the future. If I and my team judged that pupils ought to be getting a better deal – following an extremely detailed and many-faceted inspection – we would walk away from the school knowing that we had done the best job we could have done for the pupils, even though the school would have been given a grade 3 or grade 4. However, I always walked in with no fixed idea of what that school would be like, having only looked at the data. That is where I differed greatly from a few of my colleagues. Ofsted have still not sorted out that mindset in some inspectors, and that isn't good enough because it isn't fair or moral. Every school deserves to be inspected with an open mind, poor headline data or not.

Yes, things in a school may have to change. Yes, people may have to leave as a result of the inspection. It may be leaders initially, but perhaps later, under a change of leadership, teaching staff will need to go too. However, on inspection, you follow the moral imperative that the pupils come first. They only get one chance at their education, and an inspection which highlights problems in a school can help them to get the best out of the education they are offered in the years they have left there. As I observed in *Talk for Teaching*,[5] head teachers and principals are brilliant people doing an extremely difficult and demanding job – indeed, I describe them all as mad for doing the job at all – but some find that brilliance beyond them and this can impact on pupils. In that case, it doesn't matter how much effort you put into inspection preparation, this book won't save you.

In the past, I have suggested that a grade 4 and special measures is not the worst thing that can happen to a school. It used to give the school a baseline from which to change and move forward. (But does anyone like working in a school that is clearly failing? No.) However, things have changed markedly in recent years and now we have the blight of forced academisation. To force a school into a trust that they don't know and which may have an approach that parents, especially, may not want for

---

5   Paul Garvey, *Talk for Teaching: Rethinking Professional Development in Schools* (Woodbridge: John Catt, 2017).

their children is the single worst thing that can happen to a grade 4 school. To have no agency whatsoever in your future is wrong. Forced academisation is a cruel place to be. It is an ideological trap and the sooner it is removed, the better.

I believe it is time for a new kind of inspectorate, and I'm not alone. The Labour Party committed to abolishing Ofsted at their conference in September 2019 and the National Education Union (NEU) support this too. Many in education are in agreement: Ofsted have had their day. The discussions around a viable replacement are already happening. @HeadsRoundtable, on Twitter, is a collection of forward-thinking head teachers who have some excellent proposals for the future of inspection and my views are very much aligned with theirs. It is time for a change. Maybe the inspectorate's tardiness in stopping inspections at the start of the coronavirus crisis will convince schools that they may not be the force for good that they say they are.

This book is not about the future of inspection though; it is about providing schools with the best arguments for facing inspection within this framework.

If a school is not failing, but outside agencies such as the local authority or the regional school commissioner's office are applying pressure by saying that it is failing (perhaps without an actual inspection), this book will help you with your arguments. Again, it will not save you if outside agendas are fixed or if your school really is poor, but there are organisations that may be able to help – especially the NAHT (www.naht. org.uk).

Unknown unknowns

When preparing for inspection, Donald Rumsfeld's quote from 2002 rings very true. He was talking about a very different circumstance and was actually alluding to the 1955 work of two American psychologists, Joseph Luft and Harrington Ingham. His rather tortuous comment, during a Department of Defense press briefing concerning the lack of evidence for weapons of mass destruction in the Iraq War, has become infamous:

---

there are known knowns; there are things we know we know. We also know there are known unknowns; that is to say, we know there are some things we do not know. But there are also unknown unknowns – the ones we don't know we don't know.[6]

Therein lies the crux of what this book will help you to do. I have already mentioned one possible unknown unknown around the capacity for further improvement, and there will be many more. I will also expose your own unknown unknowns – those gaps in your inspection knowledge that could, potentially, cost you dearly on inspection. You will probably never know the degree to which your lack of knowledge about such unknown unknowns will have damaged your defence, if indeed they do. However, with those unknown unknowns revealed, it becomes possible for you to have the confidence to take control of your inspection and to present your arguments in the most credible way possible.

The book is divided into four main chapters:

1. Inspection Preparation

2. SEF Writing

3. An Inspector's Inspection – Inspection Methodology

4. A School's Inspection

where you will uncover the unknown unknowns bespoke to you. I can't point each one out, as your personal unknown unknowns are, logically, unknown unknowns to me too! Some information will be known to you and some you might be hoping to find out, but no one except yourself will understand when you have discovered a little nugget of an unknown unknown.

---

6   Donald H. Rumsfeld, Department of Defense news briefing (12 February 2002). Available at: https://archive.defense.gov/Transcripts/Transcript.aspx?TranscriptID=2636.

CHAPTER 1

INSPECTION PREPARATION

1.1. Be a Great School

First and foremost: be a great school. Here, I agree with Ofsted completely. If your school is a great school, you have no need to worry about Ofsted and absolutely no need to do anything extra to prepare, even for this framework. Your curriculum will stand and your leaders will be able to speak with confidence in deep dives. If this is you, please pass this book on to a school that may need it. Schools such as yours just need to carry on doing what they are doing and continuing to improve.

I know of a few schools which did not complete a self-evaluation under the previous framework. They had no need. Instead, they had a great school with excellent data to equip them with the confidence that an inspection team couldn't miss that they do things in an excellent way. Some schools may feel that way under this framework too, and good luck to them. What those schools do is nothing short of remarkable, year after year after year. There is no set pattern or format that makes them remarkable; just a vision of excellence which brings everyone on board and with the leadership to achieve a common purpose – excellent outcomes, in the widest of senses, for their pupils. That vision and common purpose leads to large and small comprehensives (with or without sixth forms) being excellent; nursery, infant, junior and primary schools being excellent; very traditional schools being excellent; Montessori schools being excellent; grammar and Steiner schools being excellent. There are examples of excellence in every type and phase of school.

There is #nobestwayoverall here (my Twitter hashtag in which I fully believe). With great vision and purpose, all schools have the potential to be excellent. In all these schools (and classrooms) there is just excellent leadership and a vision that fits the context of the school to a T. If that is you, please put this book down and do something more worthwhile. You don't need my help: you are already firmly in control!

Please just be ethical in your approach. If not, we can end up with this:

So, school improvement, in 5.

1. Take a Grade 4 school by forced academisation.
2. Impose zero tolerance.
3. Exclude all kids who can't cope (all the poorer behaved ones you don't want).
4. Off roll to home ed others in Y11.
5. Dissuade parents of SEND.

Hey presto![1]

Behaviour quickly shapes up and results, both short term and long term, are almost certain to be better than they would have been. It's a seductive method of school improvement, but is it ethical?

Better published results may produce rapid school improvement, but what about the pupils who are no longer there and would have stayed to take GCSEs under a more inclusive regime? What about their families? Or other schools that must pick up the pieces? Or the effect on the targeted pupils' mental health? Or increases in crime in local communities as the security of a caring school is gone from those young people's lives? There are serious questions to be answered by schools and trusts which pursue this route of rapid school improvement. Real school improvement for all pupils – holding fast to the faded but moral tenet of every child matters – takes time, and the inspectorate and government should recognise that and grant more time to schools in challenging circumstances and their head teachers.

Most of these schools have maintained excellence for a number of years and continue to be outstanding. But many of them have not been inspected for nearly 15 years and over 1,000 have not been inspected

---

1   See https://twitter.com/PaulGarvey4/status/1125478438490574848.

for over a decade.[2] I believe that this exemption is an anachronism that Ofsted must address. Although many of these grade 1 schools continue to be excellent, others may be developing problems that are not easily (or yet) revealed in their IDSR or known to parents. If there is no inspection of these schools, who would know before a crisis hits? It appears that outstanding schools will now be included in regular inspections from September 2020.

It is my personal belief that, if we must have Ofsted, all schools should be inspected regularly. I also believe that the outstanding grade should be removed from the Ofsted handbook. In my view, schools should be judged to be either providing a good education or not. Parents' perceptions of what is an outstanding school are often very different to the outstanding criteria set out in the handbook. If a school is judged to be providing a good standard of education, then let's allow parents to choose their school based on the information the school provides. They will have the security of Ofsted's stamp of approval, without the worry or perception that, even if a school is 'good', it could somehow still be quite a way from being 'good enough'. But, even so, that school may still turn out to be perfect for their child.

Schools also know that an outstanding badge will exempt them from inspection, as long as their pupils' outcomes remain pretty good and they have no major safeguarding issues that Ofsted judge to be 'qualifying concerns'. Such concerns are down to Ofsted to decide. There are no detailed published criteria, yet, for them. A qualifying concern would cause senior HMI to send in an inspection team.

Notwithstanding my own objections to the grade of outstanding or, indeed, the continuation of Ofsted, I am a realist. Ofsted are unlikely to disappear overnight and the badge of outstanding currently confers significant weight in MAT discussions. Hence, despite any objections to the whole process, or parts thereof, that you or I may have, this is a very good reason to be inspection-persuasive if you are a grade 2 or grade 1 cusp school. *Taking Control 2* will help schools in your position.

---

2   Daniel Wainwright, Ofsted: 1,010 'outstanding' schools not inspected for a decade, *BBC News* (2 October 2019). Available at: https://www.bbc.co.uk/news/uk-england-49579520.

1.2. Progress Since Your Last Inspection

Immediately following your inspection, ensure that you address what your inspection team asked of you. No matter what grade you received, those 'What does the school need to do to improve further?' points may come back to haunt you if you are not seen to have acted on them or if you cannot show that the school has improved. Even if you are a grade 2 school and were inspected five years ago, it would not be sensible to think that you can safely ignore these concerns. You can't.

I have to mention that you may find some silliness in certain 'points for improvement' from around five years ago. They derive from inspectors being asked to be time specific about improvement points with short time limits. We were requested to ask schools to make improvements in approximately 12–18 months. It was supposed to provide an exhortation from Ofsted that improvements should be rapid. Unfortunately, it led to the farcical situation where inspectors were writing 18-month timescales for improvement for good schools that were not going to be inspected for at least three years, and sometimes five! (This has now been changed to approximately four years.) Who would monitor the improvement (or not) at the end of the written timescale? You can safely ignore those frankly daft time limits, but you can't ignore the improvement points.

I will detail the ways in which improvement can be demonstrated throughout the book, but the points for improvement from your previous inspection need to be explained fully under a subheading in your self-evaluation. If your SEF is convincing and you can show that improvement is clear, it is highly unlikely that your HMI/Ofsted inspector will make them an area for detailed exploration. You may not even be asked about them. There will be other inspection-trail, curriculum-based fish for your inspector(s) to fry. However, if you skip over them, then you may find that you are suddenly having to scramble around for evidence to show that improvement has happened and laying yourself open to an issue that could cost you.

This is where your previous lead inspector can have been at his or her best. If you are a grade 3 or grade 4 school, the points for improvement (perhaps with some discussion) will have been set by your inspection team. They are often plentiful, often too plentiful; their number would have been determined by the writing expectations and quality assurance process. Your lead inspector will have known that any criticism of the school in the main body of the report would have to be followed up in a point for improvement, and as grade 3 and grade 4 schools often have a range of poorer areas, there may be a plethora of points for improvement.

However, if you were a grade 2 school, you (or the head teacher at the time) may well have been able to work with the lead inspector to formulate areas for improvement that were most useful to the school. This excellent approach was used by many leads. I did, and I confess that I often exchanged next-day emails with head teachers of schools I had just inspected as good or outstanding to ensure the correct wording on areas for improvement. I often found them very hard to formulate at the end of the second day when I was usually shattered and my brain was turning to mush. If your lead inspector worked with you in this way, improvements in these areas ought to be easy to evidence, as they will have been areas in which you knew you needed to improve.

If you are a grade 4 school, fight against forced academisation with everything you have got, and good luck. It's not easy but it is possible. By April 2019, 33 academy orders had been overturned in the previous three years.[3]

If you are not 'rebrokered' (Ofsted's scare quotes, not mine, in the section 8 handbook) via an academy order from the secretary of state for education, you will be subject to monitoring visits and reinspected within 30 months (para. 150, p. 37, S8). During this time, any HMI monitoring visits will assess your progress against the improvements asked for during your inspection. You must target your work towards these. Escaping from the grade 4 label has to be very high priority.

Grade 3 schools may receive monitoring visits; it depends on the grades. If leadership and management has been judged as grade 2, the Ofsted regional inspector may decide that a monitoring visit is unnecessary. The same regional director also has the power to bring the inspection forward from the usual time of within 30 months or delay it beyond 30 months, depending on what they perceive to be your rate of

---

3   Freddie Whittaker, Ministers have U-turned on 33 attempts to force schools to become academies, *Schools Week* (5 April 2019). Available at: https://schoolsweek.co.uk/ministers-have-u-turned-on-33-attempts-to-force-schools-to-become-academies.

improvement. Basically, all timings are down to Ofsted, but the usual timescale for the reinspection of requires improvement schools is within 30 months.

Whenever you are inspected, be ready. Your progress from your previous requires improvement grading needs to be carefully laid out in your SEF. Also, concentrate on demonstrating through your data that the pupils are safe and their progress is accelerating as a result of improvements to your curriculum. The farcical idea of 'coasting schools' has gone, but the handbook is clear that failure to improve could open up a grade of inadequate (para. 122, p. 31, S8).

Whatever the timing of your next inspection, it is important to target your inspection preparation work towards persuading the next lead inspector that you have made sufficient progress for them to feel that you no longer fall into the requires improvement category. Your SEF is your weapon here. As an addendum, it is possible for a school to move straight from requires improvement to outstanding. Almost any grade is possible at your next inspection. If you feel you should now be judged outstanding, or on the way to being outstanding, say so in your SEF.

If you do receive monitoring visits, they can offer a very useful and supportive process, led by some excellent HMI who really care about the improvements schools are making. Ofsted can allow time for HMI to revisit and revisit until they feel the school has improved sufficiently and is ready for a full inspection. Recently, forced inspection has got in the way of this process for some grade 4 schools, and if the school is an 'orphan' school that no sponsor wants to take on, school improvement can be badly delayed, especially if the head teacher leaves and an interim head is appointed. In this situation, schools need help. Governors and the head teacher can request a monitoring visit, but good luck in getting Ofsted to listen.

In some cases, schools which really should have had a monitoring visit have not received one. Others have only received one visit, early on in their requires improvement life. This is down to Ofsted not having enough HMI. They could have used some of their 1,500-plus other inspectors to lead those monitoring inspections, but this didn't happen for many years and was an opportunity missed. When these schools are reinspected, but have received no support and are given requires improvement again, what responsibility should Ofsted take for the grade remaining the same? These schools need help. In the past, I have been privileged to have supported some schools which have subsequently gained grade 2 at their next inspection. However, for Ofsted not to offer regular monitoring support to these schools, and also to suggest that they should not seek help from people trained in inspection procedures, in my view is unfair.

Ofsted inspectors could also provide this assistance, either inside or outside of Ofsted, but the organisation forbids them to lead this type of monitoring. In actuality, most do offer support, while the 70% of Ofsted inspectors who are senior leaders assist in their own schools, across MATs and sometimes in brokered school-to-school situations. I know they do because I work with them. Other independent inspectors offer support, but it has to be delivered well under the Ofsted radar, or else! I was found out – OK, it was a 'fair cop, guv' and led directly to me having to stop inspecting. But there are always silver linings, and parting company with Ofsted allowed me to write these books on how to prepare for inspection.

If your school is grade 4, you must target your inspection preparation mainly around the areas for further improvement that were identified by your inspection team, and such preparation has to start immediately following an inspection. If you are a grade 3 school, your improvement points must be a major pillar of your preparation, depending on how you are monitored. If you are a grade 2 school, ensure you have sufficient evidence to show improvement since your last inspection, but there is no need for these improvement points to dominate your preparation. Instead, concentrate mainly on demonstrating your curriculum progress – that current pupils are safe and making progress from their starting points.

You will see a clear theme in the previous paragraph which must occupy a very important part of the preparation for your next inspection. Alongside queen safeguarding, curriculum is now king but data is still the joker in the pack.

1.3. Why Have We Not Been Inspected Yet? (It's Down to Money, of Course!)

If we must have Ofsted, or any inspectorate, I would rather see all schools, including those given the badge of outstanding, inspected on a regular cycle, notwithstanding their data or previous grade. However, cost savings have forced Ofsted along the route of 'proportionate inspection' and legislation to make outstanding schools exempt from inspection was introduced in 2012. Section 5 legislation still expects other schools to be inspected by the end of the fifth year following their previous inspection, but Ofsted's current aim is to inspect previously good schools approximately every four years. This timescale will be tested with the size of the current workforce. This means currently there are good schools which have not been inspected for just over five years.

New schools are inspected within the first three years of opening and normally in their third year of operation. Requires improvement and inadequate schools, not subject to a forced academisation order, are inspected again within 30 months of the publication of the previous inspection report (note: not the date of the inspection).

Ofsted call this effective transfer of inspection responsibilities to an HMI's desk 'risk assessment', and they apply it to all schools, including those they deem outstanding. Ofsted apply an algorithm, which they don't make fully public, to determine whether a school is at risk. They give it the odd name of 'machine learning'. If your school is flagged, an HMI will then apply other factors to determine whether an inspection should take place. This risk assessment normally begins 'in time for the start of the third year following the last inspection' (para. 14, p. 6, S5).

If you are an outstanding or good school, then waiting for your next inspection can get wearing, even if you are exempt. I know Ofsted's view is that schools shouldn't prepare for inspection, but the schools I support feel strongly that this view is not sensible, and this view has intensified with the introduction of the 2019 EIF. I believe that Ofsted are being either naive or disingenuous in holding this view. Most schools would be mad not to prepare.

The reasons for regular changes in the dates for school inspection are obvious. It comes down to a lack of inspectors, especially HMI, and a lack of money. I predict that Ofsted will struggle to achieve the inspection time target of 'approximately four years' and, as such, grade 2 schools may well need to continue to be 'inspection ready' for a long time, often through changes of key personnel. That is difficult – unless, of course, specific preparation for your inspection is, as Ofsted would like us to believe, unnecessary.

Grade 1 schools are currently exempt from inspection, but won't be for long. If you are an outstanding school that now has waited 15 years to be inspected – and you have little idea when you will be inspected again – you will find that the inspection playing field you have to negotiate has changed considerably. New senior staff and probably a new head teacher (or a succession of several) may bring with them recent inspection experience, but in ten years a school's vision and context can change enormously. Isn't this in itself a reason to inspect outstanding schools regularly? Again, money dictates.

Although exempt might sound like an enviable place to be, if your school isn't exempt, it may not be the easiest of positions to occupy. There are outstanding schools which would like to be inspected regularly. The noose of expectation can tighten with time.

The regime of proportionate inspection was introduced in 2012. The government rationale at the time was that regular inspection was an unnecessary burden on the highest-performing schools (as determined by Ofsted). However, Estelle Morris, the then shadow education secretary, recognised that cost saving was the real driving force behind it. In 2011 she observed: 'Only the treasury benefits from the proposal to waive future inspections for schools that Ofsted judges "outstanding".'[4]

Ofsted's core funding has been reduced by £60 million (or 32%) in the ten years from 2010–2011 to 2019–2020: from £185 million to £125 million.[5] Swingeing cuts in anyone's book. In my opinion, Estelle Morris' comment remains true: since 2011, all of Ofsted's tinkering

---

4   Estelle Morris, Exempting schools from Ofsted inspection is a worrying policy, *The Guardian* (21 November 2011). Available at: https://www.theguardian.com/education/2011/nov/21/ofsted-inspections-outstanding-schools-exempt.

5   Ofsted, *Annual Report and Accounts 2018–19*. HC 2398 (2019), p. 25. Available at: https://www.gov.uk/government/publications/ofsted-annual-report-and-accounts.

with inspection timings have almost certainly been driven by a cost-saving imperative.

Never mind the outstanding schools. The current system has left some good schools without an inspection for over five years. If they convert to being an academy towards the end of that period, this may be extended further to perhaps over eight years. Is this healthy?

As a result, schools are anxious that a fairly easily explained dip in their headline data could lead to an inspection with only half a day's notice, during which they run the risk of dropping a grade because of that dip. This is still the case, even though Ofsted now say that they will inspect mainly on curriculum and not data. Data dips like this are seldom the result of a curriculum meltdown and are much more likely to be cohort specific, especially for schools in challenging circumstances. It is unlikely that machine learning takes curriculum changes into account, and neither does HMI risk-assessment. In the current high-stakes academy climate this could be catastrophic for the school. An inspection could hit at precisely the wrong time of change and the dip could be very short term, with the school recovering well. Not to prepare fully, if your previous year or two of IDSR looks poorer than previous data, could be a very risky path to take.

Ofsted examine a school's data every year in preparation for the third year following inspection. But they do not have access to all the data you would present on inspection, only the data that is publicly available. In addition, they no longer trust schools to know progress in other years, beyond the published data, from their own internal data. They make decisions based on the published data as to whether they should consider the school for early inspection and then inspect, but they don't tell you their full rationale for that inspection. Then they tell schools not to prepare for your inspection, although it may have been triggered by your data, via a risk assessment, but they won't tell you that either. Instead, Ofsted will inspect schools on the EIF, ostensibly with curriculum at the fore. But it isn't. Poor data will be driving some of these earlier-than-expected inspections. In schools in challenging circumstances that is hard, as they are still judged against all other schools by value-added data, with no reference to contextual value added.

Don't be fooled. Although data will not be at the fore during your inspection, under the EIF your lead inspector will have seen the data trends. If your inspection is early, you may know the reason, or if not, you may be easily able to infer a reason from the headline data. Your self-evaluation here is the key. Under 'impact' you can explain, concisely, any data trends and set them in context. Assuaging any worries that your lead inspector may have can be crucial. On your first day of inspection, it is far better to encounter a lead inspector with an open mind than to meet one who feels that they will need to look for holes in your curriculum to explain a poor data trend to get your report through quality assurance.

Would you expect your pupils not to prepare for their SATs, GCSEs or A levels? Not in a million years. Instead, you support those pupils in preparing for their tests. I believe that advising schools not to prepare for inspection is an untenable position for Ofsted to take. I support Ofsted in some areas, but this is one where I definitely cannot agree. Not all schools need to prepare, but most do. If your school is one of them, I hope this book helps you greatly in doing so.

1.4. School Reviews and Mocksteds – an External Eye, or Not

As part of your preparation, you may feel it is useful to get an external view on your school. There is nothing wrong with this and it is best done as part of your self-evaluation cycle or school improvement plan, so all leaders and staff are used to the process. However, for such a review to be a 'mocksted' (an Ofsted invention for a review that mimics inspection) only puts extra pressure on classroom teachers and subject leaders. There are horror stories doing the rounds about what schools are imposing on their staff in order to prepare for the inspection framework because they are so worried by the whole process.

These worries are completely understandable, and Ofsted are showing scant regard for the huge volume of extra work that this framework is creating, but this depth of preparation is unnecessary and wrong. I will detail how I think you should prepare throughout this book, and I hope it will help to put your mind at rest as to the type of preparation you need to do. Focus on what will be useful, while limiting impact on your classroom teachers as far as you can. Your SEF is a big part of this preparation: see Chapter 2 on SEF preparation and my dialogic SEF tools for primary and secondary in the appendices.

I have never been in favour of mocksteds. They are dreadful things for classroom teachers because staff effectively end up being inspected twice. Information on what to do to prepare can be given around a table by a well-informed adviser who has a good feel for the school and where it is. Or schools can save themselves the cost of even that and prepare themselves, using this book or any other good source of advice. Methodology mirrors like mocksteds create unnecessary and sometimes extreme amounts of work. Don't do one!

With luck, and if you are not already an academy, your local authority may have good people who can review your school well, and may even be able to review it as part of an annual cycle. However, they can have agendas around inspection – and might even rely on a mocksted approach to review your school. They can also be very defensive when writing review reports and judging grades, ensuring their own backs are covered. This can be damaging because inspectors will want to see the outcomes of any external reviews. Some strong and successful local authorities can stand up to outside influences better than others, and I know of some excellent individuals who still work in the sector. Other good quality local authorities work well and in tandem with their regional schools commissioner and that relationship is set to develop further.

Nevertheless, some schools tell awful stories about weak local authorities. Tales of a lack of support, unfair grades the school doesn't agree with and draining improvement plans abound. No wonder local government is weak: budget cuts have forced many smaller authorities to shrink their school services so that almost no one is left. Without enough personnel, these authorities commission much of their school monitoring and improvement work from teaching schools or outside agencies. Weaker local authorities will roll over and do the regional schools commissioner's bidding, so the pressures on officers can be great. Variations in the quality of government have never been greater, and in my opinion funding cuts are to blame. As a school, you will know the level of monitoring and help that your own local authority provides. However, there are times when your governing body has to stand up and say no to the extra workload of such monitoring. In the end, who is the monitoring for? How much does it benefit your school and your pupils? If you can, refuse mocksteds from outside agencies or your local authority.

MATs have taken over the monitoring role from local authorities in their trusts, and some feel they must monitor using internal mocksteds, often led by their own senior leaders who are Ofsted trained. If you are reading this as the CEO of a MAT and you truly care about your staff, please don't go down this route. You can help your schools to prepare very well without it. In general (though not always), schools themselves find it very difficult to say no to the wishes of their trust, so I'm addressing you on their behalf: no more mocksteds!

Another plea from me to head teachers: there is absolutely no need to provide your inspection team with indications of teacher quality. All references to this in this framework have gone and the grade for 'quality of teaching' is now subsumed into 'quality of education'. Thank goodness. I argued for the removal of the grade for quality of teaching in *Taking Control* and that request was made by many others too. Please don't use any of the bullet points in the new section 5 handbook to create a checklist for your teachers, so you can somehow judge how well they are doing their jobs. Head teachers and senior leaders know where there is excellent teaching, they know where there is pretty good teaching and they know who are the (usually very few) teachers who need ongoing support. There is no need whatsoever to grade your teachers. None.

1.5. Curriculum is the New King, Safeguarding is Still Queen, But Data is the Joker in the Pack[6]

'Some things change, some stay the same', sang The Pretenders in 'Hymn to Her' back in 1986, and it could describe the EIF perfectly. An understanding of what I mean by that will inform your preparation and set you on your guard, especially if you are in a school in challenging circumstances.

Ofsted say that the curriculum is the substance of education (para. 169, p. 41, S5) and they have fashioned a framework around that belief. I don't believe it is. I believe that every child matters is what education is about, but I think that Ofsted have completely lost sight of Every Child Matters. Every Child Matters is not even mentioned in the new framework or in any of the handbooks. If I were HMCI, this framework would look very different and would put children at its heart. However, those beliefs are neither here nor there, and the realist in me has written this book.

References to curriculum, not surprisingly, dominate the handbooks, although the quality of a school's curriculum is not a limiting judgement for achieving a grade. Only the effectiveness of safeguarding limits a grade, beyond the four main judgement areas. Published reports, especially grade 2 reports, usually explain weaknesses by referring to curriculum problems, particularly around progression in the curriculum and more especially in foundation subjects. Never has the spotlight shone so brightly on subjects outside of mathematics, English and science! Very often these perceived curriculum weaknesses are linked to weaknesses in published results in requires improvement reports. When you see comments like 'Pupils do not achieve well in mathematics', 'Pupils now make more progress in reading, writing and mathematics than in previous years' and 'Results at the end of Year 11 have not been

---

6   Don't you just love trying to find the correct grammatical use of 'data' in an idiom or otherwise! I go with the *Guardian*'s style guide here. 'Data takes a singular verb (like agenda), though strictly a plural; no one ever uses "agendum" or "datum"': https://www.theguardian.com/guardian-observer-style-guide-d. Ofsted agree with this use in their house style: https://www.gov.uk/government/uploads/system/uploads/attachment_data/file/596603/GuideToOfstedHouseStyle.pdf. If, for you, data takes a plural verb then 'data are king' is correct, but for me 'data is the joker', even though my grammar check hates it!

strong but they are improving', you know that published results are influencing inspector opinions. This concerns me, and my worries centre on the weight that inspectors still give to progress measures and, now that the focus is apparently off academic progress, attainment measures.

Progress

It is worth stopping here and considering the references to progress in the EIF. Ofsted's focus shows changes from the previous framework but, as I have said, some things remain the same. It is confusing at best.

In Years 5–11 most references are to progress in knowledge, understanding and skills in subjects (e.g. para. 87, p. 24, S5; para. 97, p. 26, S5). However, in early years and in sixth-form provision, reference is made to progress from starting points to end points – for example, evaluating the quality of early years provision (para. 284, p. 77, S5) and the grade descriptors for evaluating sixth-form provision (p. 85, S5). The Progress 8 accountability measure is only mentioned twice in the section 5 handbook (both times in relation to it not being of much use!): for some special educational needs and disability (SEND) pupils in special schools (p. 92) and to university technical colleges (p. 91). However, achievement is mentioned, or inferred, in every grade descriptor for impact, especially for SEND and disadvantaged pupils (pp. 49–52). For me, the key phrase appears in the impact descriptor for good under 'quality of education' (p. 51; my emphasis):

Pupils develop detailed knowledge and skills across the curriculum and, *as a result*, achieve well. This is reflected in results from national tests and examinations that meet government expectations, or in the qualifications obtained.

Do pupils really achieve well because of this alone? I very much doubt it, but it is what Ofsted believe and hence how you should prepare for your inspection. Make sure that you point out where your outcomes are the result of curriculum improvements (whether you feel they are or they aren't) at every opportunity. Help your lead inspector to write their report.

EIF: what's really important?

The EIF paints a picture that, on the surface, sends a message to schools that they will be judged on progress within subjects and beyond, in the curriculum in its widest sense, and that via this curriculum progress a school's outcome will be improved achievement. However, this is certain to be more difficult in schools with disadvantaged catchments. Not impossible, but much more difficult. Everything is harder for these schools. Much has been written on this and much has been ignored in the research that Ofsted have conducted. Value-added progress is discriminatory to schools in challenging circumstances and ignores these difficulties, so this measure of quality of education is flawed and unfair.

For all schools, and especially those schools in challenging areas, where published results may show attainment weaknesses because of the starting points of the pupils, ignore your data at your peril, for it may well come back and bite you.[7] The SEF is your vehicle to explain and persuade, and the 'impact' section under 'quality of education' is now the place to explain pupil outcomes from the previous framework.

In the framework's previous iteration, Ofsted tried, in vain, to convince us that leadership and management were, effectively, the substance of education and that this was the key to good outcomes. In the end they abandoned the effort. It was the first judgement area in the previous section 5 handbook and the HMCI at the time, Sir Michael Wilshaw, was

---

7   For those who say, 'Every child should be able to achieve and no child's expectations should be capped,' of course! Surely everyone in education would agree, but to attempt to ignore the huge difficulties of children and families in schools in challenging circumstances, by using value-added data, is tantamount to condemning more schools than necessary to requires improvement because of their catchments. These schools attempt to counter George W. Bush's 'soft bigotry of low expectations' (a phrase coined by his main scriptwriter and outspoken evangelical, Michael Gerson) every day in their work, and they don't strive to fail. See Office of the Press Secretary, President Bush Addresses NAACP Annual Convention, Washington (20 July 2006). Available at: https://georgewbush-whitehouse.archives.gov/news/releases/2006/07/20060720.html.

However, Ofsted fail to give these schools the safety of good again and again, and the percentage of schools in challenging circumstances in requires improvement is higher than the percentage of advantaged schools in requires improvement. In addition, the percentage of schools in challenging circumstances that are outstanding is far lower than their advantaged equivalents. Attainment still clearly rules progress for Ofsted in these schools and even progress measures are stacked against them as value-added compared to all schools.

very clear that quality of leadership and management was the central pillar of school improvement. We now have a new HMCI and a new framework: Amanda Spielman believes that curriculum should be central, and Ofsted have had to follow. Some things have definitely changed here: Ofsted have swung more towards traditional and, it could be argued, conservative educational values. Nevertheless, I believe that the difference between grade 2 and grade 3 (and therefore overall effectiveness) has stayed the same. It appears in the framework in the descriptor I highlighted on page 31 (p. 51). A lead inspector will struggle to rate your school good, great curriculum or not, if your published results are not what they deem to be good enough. Where are the benchmarks? There aren't any. Inspection is subjective. It depends on the mindset of the lead inspector and their team. So, *take control* and influence that mindset!

During inspection, data used to be king and safeguarding was queen. Well, safeguarding is still queen – and I have little sympathy if you don't get that right. But while curriculum is Ofsted's new king, data is the joker in the pack, and it could trip you up if your published results are not considered good enough and you are not prepared. This won't be a surprise to most schools and probably not to you as a reader. Ofsted were unsuccessful in convincing schools of the paramountcy of leadership and management in inspectors' thinking in the previous framework; I think they will struggle to convince schools who have 'questionable' data of the paramountcy of curriculum in the EIF.

Your lead inspector will receive your most recent IDSR as part of their preparatory information from Ofsted. Everything else that an inspector receives, pre-inspection, is listed in the handbook (para. 65, p. 19, S5). If your results are deemed good enough by your lead inspector, the inspection will very likely be about how the curriculum has been a central plank in supporting those good results. No doubt about it. The deep dives will be thorough, and if they produce the results you want, you are likely to feel they have been fair. Of course, those deep dives may still raise concerns for inspectors around curriculum progression through your school, despite your published results. Good results alone will not grant you security from a grade 3 for overall effectiveness – and this book will not help you to convince them of the cogency of your curriculum. However, if your lead inspector has pre-inspection worries about your results, the inspection may be about the team finding enough problems with your curriculum to justify a grade 3 for quality of education. Believe me, after inspecting for more than 11 years, I know how possible that is.

Exactly the same outcomes (and curriculum) could produce one grade or another from two different lead inspectors/HMI. That is a fact. Prepare, and prepare well, to persuade them to go for the higher grade, and don't leave an explanation of your pupil outcomes out of your preparation.

Internal progress and assessment data

Ofsted state that inspectors won't use non-statutory internal progress and assessment data. Indeed, they have created a separate subheading (paras 194–196, p. 47, S5) to tell you they won't. Inspectors are sticking to the script here and are not asking schools for such data. Instead, they say that inspectors will only use 'officially generated national data' (e.g. para. 197, p. 48, S5) – that is, the published data. But don't let that put you off *presenting* such data. If your internal data clearly indicates progress in all years and is cogent, who are Ofsted to deny you your pride in showing this off?

There is nothing wrong with presenting this information in your SEF and also talking it through on inspection. The inspectors can't help but listen. Although they will not mention it in any report, it may help them in their personal deliberations about how good the school is, even though they will claim that they won't consider it. Set it in the context of how much your excellent, progressive and knowledge-rich curriculum is shining through in the work being done in each year group. Make sure the team see this progress in current work in books and when talking to a range of stakeholders, including the pupils. A lead inspector may try to stop you referring to the data, but be strong. If you want them to see it, they should not prevent you from showing them. Say, 'With respect, we feel this data is important in telling our story to date …' and carry on. *Take control.*

1.6. Pre-inspection – Your Inspection Action Plan

An inspection plan that you can put into action as soon as the first call comes in from Ofsted is well worth the work. Here is an anonymised example from a real primary school. Whether you are a primary or secondary school, I'm sure you will want to produce something similar.

_____ **Primary School**

An Inspector Calls ...

Ofsted Phone Call Checklist

We only have a few hours to go to showcase our amazing school. Essentially, we need to be ready to show off all the great things we do and be able to talk about the things that make _____ Primary School great. While we should be ever-ready to show off our school, we do require some preparation ahead of the impending inspection.

Action	Responsible*	Complete
IMMEDIATE/ASAP		
Call a staff briefing at the earliest opportunity to inform staff – issue staff guidance sheets and key information (e.g. timetable, any lines of enquiry).	Fred	
Notify parents/carers via text, Twitter and website.	Office	
Notify governors and trust CEO/central team and any part-time staff.	Enid	

Action	Responsible*	Complete
Review and collect class timetables, cancel any cover teaching/PPA (to be rearranged) and brief additional staff where support is required.		
Notify and brief relevant wider staff team (e.g. kitchen staff, peripatetic music teachers, volunteers).	Zephyr	
Diary check (including cancellation of any non-urgent appointments for head teacher).	PA	
Arrange and prepare a base room for inspectors (conference room) with refreshments (including lunch), along with fob and key access.	Donald	
Arrange late locking of school and order pizzas for staff working late.	Donald	
PRIOR TO INSPECTION		
Checks: School walk – environment check: display, clutter, etc.	Enid	

Action	Responsible*	Complete
Site walk – cleanliness, tidiness, litter, etc.	Zephyr	
Brief lunchtime supervisors and check rotas and timetables, etc.	Bert	
Organisational: Prepare map of school, staff list, relevant network access, etc. Prepare governors' minutes and liaise with the head teacher to arrange timetable for CEOP (Child Exploitation and Online Protection) and other governors to visit. Ensure IT team are available on-site for day of inspection.	Donald	
Safeguarding: Prepare the single central record; ensure site risk-assessments, accident books, staff files and inventory have been updated. Ensure training record, safeguarding audit and PREVENT action plan have been updated. Final reminders about security (including IT) and safety procedures.	Zephyr	

Action	Responsible*	Complete
Assessment: Prepare and collate data summaries, case studies, analysis and any other key documents (e.g. pupil premium plan).	Enid	
School improvement and curriculum: Prepare and collate any key documents and information related to school improvement (e.g. SEF/SDP/RAP overview).	Fred	
Brief safeguarding leads and ensure curriculum overviews and class timetables are up to date. Ensure sport premium plan is up to date and available.	Mendelssohn	
Children: Call the children together for an assembly to notify them of the visit and remind them of core values, behaviours and vision.	Team leaders	
School council meeting – what have been our priorities?	Zephyr	

Action	Responsible*	Complete
Every Child Matters: Ensure case studies are available and assessment data is prepared. Brief teaching assistants about inspection and ECM meeting about role during visit. Final check of provision map, pupil passports and ECM records.	Piper	
SLT briefing (4pm) to discuss: Final check of books. Key information to be ready and available. Curriculum overview – what is our story? Key assessment briefing.	SLT	
Finance and personnel: Check employee files are organised and up to date. Ensure recruitment paperwork is organised and available (including those who were rejected during selection processes). Prepare overview of budget to date.	Donald	

Action	Responsible*	Complete
Office check and briefing – organisation, confidentiality, etc.		
Other: Ensure exercise books are prepared and available. Ensure planning is available (normal planning). Ensure class information folders are up to date. Staff well-being: ensure they feel calm and prepared.	Team leaders	
DURING INSPECTION		
Ensure orderly behaviour around school (corridors, playground, dining room) and make sure specific areas are looked after (e.g. library).	All	
Check for litter, cleanliness and organisation during the day.	All	
Ensure security adherence (e.g. ID badges worn at all times).	All	
Ensure tightness in timetables and time-keeping.	All	

Action	Responsible*	Complete
Ask inspectors for their ID badge (to confirm they are Ofsted) and issue a green lanyard.	Ermintrude	
Be visible as much as possible – playground with parents, dining room, breaktimes, lunchtimes, etc.	All	
Shine! Be the stars we know you are – relax and enjoy!	All	

*All names have been changed, of course!

1.7. Pre-inspection – Self-Evaluation and the Importance of Your SEF

Chapter 2 is all about writing your SEF and there are dialogic tools to help both primary and secondary schools to write self-evaluations in the appendices. These should be used in tandem with Chapter 2.

Your self-evaluation is the main chance you have to set your curriculum and data in the context of your pupils and school. If you write your SEF in convincing and proud language, it should already have made a big difference to your lead inspector's thinking before they walk through the doors of your school. I have already remarked that this book can't save you if you aren't doing a good enough job, but the information here about self-evaluation will go a long way towards helping you to present the most credible arguments that you can. This is especially true if you are a 'cusp' school (i.e. you could easily be one grade or another according to Ofsted handbook criteria – grade 2/3 is a crucial cusp). Always remember: all judgements are subjective and it is possible to sway the thinking of a lead inspector.

CHAPTER 2

SEF WRITING

2.1. Writing a Persuasive Self-Evaluation

For me, an SEF has only one purpose: to put an idea into the mind of your lead inspector that you deserve the grade for overall effectiveness that you believe you are worth.

Do evaluate your school regularly. Do update your SEF regularly as a result. Do use your SEF as a working document, with stakeholders, to see the positives about where you are and where you are going. But, don't forget that your SEF will have a singular audience on the afternoon prior to your inspection. For me, you are writing your SEF primarily to persuade your lead inspector, and any other use of your SEF is secondary to that.

It is a view that will come as a surprise or even a shock to some, and one that Ofsted probably won't like, but it is a view developed from working with several hundred schools on self-evaluation and Ofsted preparation. It is also a view developed from inspecting many schools. Your SEF is crucial to your preparation and also to your lead inspector's preparation. It can put you at a disadvantage if your SEF is written naively or badly. Inspectors are human and they will make mental judgements when reading it.

Please get someone to proofread your SEF. I have read some shockers when inspecting which have been littered with spelling and grammatical errors. It's not that leaders' grammar is poor, it's just a lack of proofreading in a large document. Everyone makes mistakes, but many bad mistakes sets a poor example for school leadership whose job it is to encourage good English and grammar among pupils via drafting, checking and redrafting. Be humble and get someone to proofread your SEF for you.

I have also read SEFs that were shockers in a different way – that told me about the school's every weakness in great detail. Both types influence inspectors, but when I have seen examples of the latter, I have just smiled and thought, 'Thank you very much!' and devised my inspection trails accordingly. Neither would affect my eventual judgements, but you don't know your lead inspector's possible prejudices and how your SEF might just spark them. Although inspector quality may have increased following the 2015 cull and the change to inspectors being contracted directly to Ofsted, but why even risk such a thing? Write your SEF intelligently and cleverly to persuade, and then get a 'gatekeeper' to check it. A member of staff from the English department, your deputy or a Year 6 teacher is usually a safe bet.

An SEF must be honest but only up to a point: your SEF should not present your lead inspector with their inspection trails on a platter. Let them work for those. Use and update your self-evaluation regularly. Every good school evaluates their progress – it is a necessary element of school improvement – but have the overall SEF purpose firmly in mind throughout those evaluations. Set up a template that can be very quickly updated, almost immediately, following your initial phone call.

In my view, your self-evaluation should sit alongside your school development plan (SDP), but definitely should not be combined with it. Your SDP will include your main areas of focus, as well as your action planning and evaluation of where you are in achieving those plans, and these will give inspection trails to your lead inspector.

Ofsted will want you to make your SDP available by 8am on the morning of inspection (para. 53, p. 16, S5), but use that timing to your advantage. It is not one of the four things the lead inspector would like to see 'as early as possible to aid preparation' (para. 61, p. 18, S5; original emphasis). Thus, the timing of when you send both your SEF and SDP to your lead inspector is up to you. I would have your SEF ready to send almost as soon as the phone call with your lead inspector is finished, but I would delay sending your SDP. Don't leave it until the last minute though – if I was your lead inspector I would be annoyed by that, as I would want to read it pre-inspection. However, a gap of a few hours, sent together with all the other information you have been asked for, would give your lead inspector enough time to read your SEF first.

Ofsted say that 'any assessment [i.e. your self-evaluation] provided should be part of the school's business processes and not be generated solely for inspection purposes' (para. 47, p. 15, S5). But in all likelihood, of course, your self-evaluation will have been updated regularly and used for different purposes (do say that this is the case). What your lead inspector won't know is that you have had him or her in mind all the time. It would be a brave lead inspector who attempted to downgrade a school because they had gone against Ofsted's advice and actually prepared for their inspection! To my knowledge, it has never happened and I can't see how it ever could. However, you will be expected to show your lead inspector that you have an accurate understanding of your school's effectiveness. Aim for that phrase, or something similar, to appear in your inspection report. If it does, you will have been successful in writing a clever, intelligent and persuasive SEF and, more importantly, your school will have gained the grade you felt it deserved.

To achieve the goal of an accurate self-evaluation, don't over-egg the pudding. If you aren't worth the grades you have put in each section of your SEF, no lead inspector is going to be persuaded by what you have written. They won't believe you. However, if you believe strongly that your school is worth a particular grade, but your lead inspector could cast an ounce of possible doubt on that belief, especially via your most recent IDSR, then having a credible SEF can tip the balance in your favour. Having supported many schools with writing their self-evaluations and seeing post-inspection feedback from many other schools that have used my dialogic tools to write their SEF, the weight of evidence points firmly to this being the case.

After many of those inspections, our aim was achieved and the lead inspector wrote in the report that the school had evaluated itself accurately. If those inspectors only knew how those schools had wrestled with their conservatism! School leaders are naturally shy about saying how good their school is. Many were initially reluctant to push for something more, even though their data showed that they were better than they thought they were. In all these cases, what they needed to do was to go for the higher of two grades, or for a split grade, and back their judgement to the hilt. I'm glad to say that is exactly what they did. If they had gone for a lower grade, I feel it is likely that a percentage of those schools would be requires improvement now instead of good and others would be good instead of outstanding. It is far easier for a lead inspector to agree with a school's judgement, when the school says confidently that its judgement is accurate and it backs that up with compelling and data-rich arguments, than it is to find fault with the school's judgement and downgrade it as a result.

The person leading your inspection is human. They are faced with interpreting a set of subjective criteria. From these criteria, they are expected to determine a judgement that is a best fit to a grade. There are no benchmarks for what makes a school good. There are no Ofsted determinants which state that a certain percentage of criteria met equals one grade or another. Most importantly, there is nothing to say that a set of IDSR or other data is sufficient, or insufficient, to point to a particular judgement grade. For this reason, it is possible, with the right approach, to nudge your lead inspector towards a desired position, and clever schools do exactly that. Your SEF is the next step towards achieving that goal, following your 90-minute phone call.

When writing your SEF, your aim is to remove as many doubts as you can from your lead inspector's mind before they sign into your school at 8am on the day of the inspection. A lead inspector who is thinking along the same lines as you will give you a far easier time on inspection than one who enters your school doubting your self-evaluation. Don't leave it to chance that alignment between the inspection team and your school will happen during the inspection. Influence that agreement beforehand. Make it as difficult as you can for your lead inspector to judge you differently to your own assessment, without an enormous effort of will and/or skill on their part.

In section 8 inspections, the handbook used to say, 'The HMI will start the short inspection from the assumption that the school remains good.'[1] This is no longer the case with the new, longer two-day version section 8 as contained in the EIF. Section 8 inspections, which most schools will receive, are effectively section 5 inspections in practice and methodology. However, following a section 8, you will receive one of four outcomes: three letters or a conversion to a graded section 5 to look at inadequate (para. 72, p. 18, S8).

---

1   Ofsted, *School Inspection Handbook – Section 8* [withdrawn]. Ref: 150077 (2018), para. 56, p. 16. Available at: https://www.gov.uk/government/publications/handbook-for-short-monitoring-and-unannounced-behaviour-school-inspections.

If you are a good school undergoing a section 8, a big aim of the SEF is to have at least an 'outcome 1' (which continues good) or perhaps an 'outcome 2' (come back and look at outstanding within one to two years). If you are an outstanding school undergoing a section 8, an outcome 1 would be great – it continues outstanding. The award of outstanding in the EIF is very different to how this was awarded in other frameworks, however, and it looks to be far harder to gain. Inspection results will show whether that is the case. An 'outcome 3' letter would mean a return within one to two years because there has been a decline in standards (the same as for good schools) whereas an 'outcome 4' would mean a conversion to section 5 within 48 hours to look at requires improvement (or worse). For a good school, an outcome 4 would be a disastrous conversion, within 48 hours, to look at the possibility of a decline to inadequate. A convincing SEF can help you to get the outcome you feel you should have and reduce the possibility of Ofsted leaving you with an outcome you really don't want.

Take control of your inspection right from the word go. Produce a convincing, cogent and proud self-evaluation which has the power to persuade your lead inspector that you should have another three years (or more) to continue as a good or outstanding school which is capable of further improvement. As well as you being happy, if your inspector can judge you accordingly and can be helped to have a cohesive evidence base to corroborate the report they will have to write the next day, I can assure you that they will leave in a happy frame of mind too.

If you are a good school that has improved since the time of your last inspection to become, in your view, an outstanding school, put that idea into your lead inspector's mind pre-inspection, via your SEF, then hit them with all guns blazing on the first morning of your section 8 inspection. Before January 2018, conversions of short section 8 inspections could take place immediately to look at a grade of outstanding. This is no longer the case, and the best you can hope for is an outcome 2 letter.

I think this is a shame and a mistake. If a good school has improved to meet the criteria for outstanding at the time of their section 8 inspection, they should have the potential to be judged so and not have to wait 12 to 24 months to receive that judgement. Still, we have what we have and, as ever, these possibilities have been limited by money and personnel.

Should I play it safe or aim for the higher of two potential grades?

If you are undecided which grade to aim for, go for the higher grade or, alternatively, sow the idea in your lead inspector's mind that you *may* be the higher grade by giving a split grade. It depends on the strength of your data. Set out your stall first: state what grade of school you believe you are and then use every word of your SEF to back up that grade. Send a clear and powerful message to the reader in the first words of your SEF: 'We believe we are a good school,' 'We believe we are at least a good school' or 'We believe we are now an outstanding school'. You are effectively saying, 'We know our school – prove us wrong.'

In the case of you stating, 'We believe we are at least a good school,' you are first of all precluding requires improvement by suggesting either grade 1 or grade 2. You are also introducing the possibility of outstanding. There is nothing wrong with doing this, especially if you feel that your curriculum improvements, combined with your improving results and behaviour, set you clearly as a good school, but there may be significant elements of better within that data. If your HMI then feels you are not yet an outstanding school, the monitoring letter will contain many positives that you can work with and use both in your next inspection and also with stakeholders, especially MAT representatives, to show your strengths.

A split grade can also tilt the thinking of your lead inspector in your favour and can be a subtle and clever way of nudging them to consider grade 1. You may get a lead inspector who is very sympathetic to your position, especially if you are a school that takes from a challenging or disadvantaged catchment. If you see this kind of thinking beginning to develop in your lead inspector, play on the difficulty that changes to the framework since the last inspection have caused and how you are a little unsure of your current grade (say 'Can anyone be truly sure, pre-inspection?'). Then push your positives even harder. If you end up as grade 2, no one can say you didn't evaluate your school correctly or that you didn't try hard for an outcome 1 letter. Precluding requires improvement sends a message of confidence. You are saying to your section 8 inspectors that it's not worth them considering a grade below and you are going to say exactly why you may even be a grade above.

However, if you feel you have improved significantly from your good position at the last inspection and you are now clearly outstanding, say, 'We believe we are now an outstanding school,' and never let go from that SEF position all through your section 8 visit. If you are sensing agreement with your assessment – and that sense of agreement may come early if your data is excellent – empathise and agree with any terms or speech that may suggest grade 1. Take every opportunity to remind your lead inspector that outstanding is no more than a best fit in each set of grade criteria. Also talk about your confidence that you can improve even further and that outstanding is, to you, just an Ofsted station on the journey to excellence in all areas. Use phrases that will speak of ambition to your lead inspector. Show that you are well aware of the existence of some schools that are far better than Ofsted outstanding and you want to be one of them. An outcome 2 letter is still your best possible outcome (an immediate conversion to a section 5 is extremely unlikely), but your letter will reflect your lead inspector's very positive opinion of your school, and Ofsted may come back early in that time-frame if the report from your lead inspector is glowing.

If you feel you are a cusp school, it is my opinion that you should always write your SEF to the grade above rather than be conservative. The reason is that your lead inspector will always find it easier to agree with what you have written. Disagreement is more difficult, but they will be skilled at interpreting your information and, depending on their experience, will be strong in their dialogue. Remember that there are no benchmarks and you must have enough ammunition to defend your position. The situation to aim for is one where you know more about what your curriculum and data say than the person leading your inspection.

If everything points to requires improvement, you clearly can't do any of this, so don't try: 'We feel we are still a school that requires improvement, but we are moving towards good.' If this is you, accept where you are and describe building from your present position. Mention the green shoots of recovery that are already there and that you are only just starting to reap the rewards of the curriculum improvements you have put in place. Be honest about the unfortunate reasons why you feel you are in this position, which may well be down to leadership changes and less skilled teaching in the past. A former grade of requires improvement is often down to changes in leadership, with the new leadership not yet having had enough time to effect change. If you feel this reflects your position, stress the recent improvements but accept the weaknesses. Grade 3 is better than grade 4, awarded because you don't know your school and perhaps because you don't have sufficient capacity for improvement. In addition, a grade 3 report containing green shoots of progress may keep the regional schools commissioner from your door for long enough for you to choose your future, rather than have it forced upon you in compulsory academisation.

A split grade 3/2 is not an impossible choice, but it is hard to justify a split-grade standpoint in this scenario. If your school is good at present, and you are having a section 8 inspection, I wouldn't recommend opting for a split grade. The only caveat is if there have been significant, positive changes in leadership after a steep dip, leading to very recent strong but uneven improvements. In this case, state that you acknowledge the past and the effect this has had, but the present leadership can't be responsible for those problems and is beginning to effect some significant improvements. In this case, a split grade and an outcome 3 letter would allow you to continue an improvement agenda, with some positive report comments. It would also help to keep the wolf of a grade 4 outcome from your door.

Schools must foresee the possible consequences of these outcomes and governors have to be aware of their options. As such, don't be afraid of talking to other academies or MATs while continuing to make improvements to pupil progress within your own school. Don't leave the issue to be forced by a section 8 lead inspector who doesn't believe in your capacity for further improvement, converts your inspection to look at inadequate and then brings in a section 5 inspection team who confirm it. Determine your own future while you still have the chance to do so. Joining a trust will hopefully give you extra time to ensure that your data is strong. It may be just what you need – a trust that allows a large element of continued independence. A 'Borg trust' (see page 51), joined via forced academisation, won't allow continued independence. Your 'old' school may improve, but it is by no means certain, and it may well improve without being forced to join such a trust.

For someone like me who supports schools for a living, those were difficult words to write. The pressures on governing bodies in schools determined to be failing to academise are huge – and if recent school changes have left you vulnerable to grade 4, or even grade 3, I feel you should consider pre-emptive action, even though the future with the MAT that you choose is, in itself, an unknown unknown.

Many MATs provide safe havens, and I have worked with some terrific trusts. However, other trusts can make previously proud and independent schools feel like they are being assimilated into the 'Borg' (an alien group from *Star Trek* who co-opt other species and technologies aligning them to their own). Joining a MAT will usually give your school two or three more years in which to demonstrate improvement, and you may get excellent help from your new trust. If MAT negotiations are well advanced, Ofsted and the regional schools commissioner (RSC) will be in contact with each other and your possible imminent inspection may be delayed, although a 2017 parliamentary report was damning about this relationship, stating: 'The relationship between Ofsted and RSCs, both nationally and regionally, remains unsatisfactory.'[2]

If you know that grade 4, or even grade 3, is a possibility at your next inspection, my advice, notwithstanding the leap into the dark that this entails, is to choose a MAT while you can rather than wait to be pushed.

If you are thinking that your current information is not looking strong enough for grade 2, you can be sure that your lead inspector will be thinking that too. In this case, grade 3 is clearly a far better option than inadequate. If you end up in special measures (inadequate and judged not to have sufficient capacity to improve) you will be forced to academise, with few choices. Your regional schools commissioner will effectively control your future. Thus, write your SEF to a grade 3, strongly countering those grade 4 bullets in the handbook and stressing any areas where you may actually fulfil some grade 2 criteria. These will exist – there are a lot of elements to the grade descriptors. If you can convince your lead inspector that you are not a failing school and there are some clear areas where you are improving, or even good, then requires improvement is a far better position to be in than special measures, although I'm afraid that both grades will put you at risk of academisation being forced upon you.

---

2   Select Committee on Education, *Multi-Academy Trusts*, 27 February 2017, HC 204 2016–17. Available at: https://publications.parliament.uk/pa/cm201617/cmselect/cmeduc/204/20403.htm.

You may settle happily for a grade 2 in a split-grade grade 1/2 scenario, but I doubt you would be as happy to settle for a grade 3 if you have been grade 2 before and you are currently not sure your where your school sits. In this case, if your situation suggests cusp grade 2/3, go for a clear good, be confident that you should remain a good and do all you can to persuade your lead inspector that this is the case. Stress all the positives. Use the grade 2 lifelines that I will refer to in sections 2.2 and 2.3. Commend to your inspectors your green shoots of progress in curriculum and data. Play on the leadership changes that now give you such excellent potential. In other words, show your lead inspector that you have the capacity for future improvement, despite a recent rocky spell not of your making. If your arguments don't work, at least you tried, and there is always a chance they will.

At this stage, I will temporarily split my narrative into primary (including infant, junior and middle schools) and secondary to discuss quality of education. There are overlaps between the two descriptions which will require some repetition, so please skip whichever part doesn't apply to you. The next sections are best read in conjunction with either the primary or secondary SEF dialogic tools in the appendices. These will talk you through how to write a self-evaluation and are designed to be stand-alone documents. Sections 2.2 to 2.7 will add some flesh to the bones of these tools.

Always have a copy of the relevant Ofsted handbook open in your browser or at your side as you write and refer to apposite parts of it in your SEF.

Coronavirus update

Schools are doing remarkable and often brave things to cope with the epidemic. There will be a chance to write these into your SEF, so take the opportunity to show the inclusive work you have undertaken. Schools are worth much more than is detailed in the EIF.

2.2. Primary Self-Evaluation

You can find the primary self-evaluation dialogic tool in Appendix 1. Use that tool, in conjunction with the advice in this chapter, to write your self-evaluation. While writing, have the Ofsted handbook with you and quote from it, where necessary, to illustrate the evidence for your grade judgement. I won't reiterate everything that is in the primary SEF tool guidance here, but I will refer to the relevant sections.

Here is a summary of what you should include in the first section of your SEF:

- Set out your grade stall (e.g. 'We believe we are a good school') right from the start. Be clear on this and use the rest of the SEF to support this statement.

- Set your school in an Ofsted grade context and then in your local context. Provide evidence of how you have translated your vision to all leaders and staff here (see section 2.6 for more on this).

- Provide information about your school using your last inspection report as your template. The 'information about your school' section no longer appears in the EIF, but it is worth using this subheading to give your inspectors a fuller idea of your school.

- Show how you have met the key issues from your previous inspection.

Following this introductory part, there is no doubt that the most important section of your primary SEF is your 'quality of education' section and the 3I's: intent, implementation and impact. I will provide advice around other sections when the secondary advice re-joins my narrative, but I will concentrate on this here. As we saw in Chapter 1, curriculum is now king but data is the joker in the pack, and I will offer plenty of tips on how you can use both to best effect.

Quality of education

Make no mistake, Ofsted are looking for a particular approach with regard to curriculum intent and implementation. Impact remains similar to what it was in the previous framework, so organise your SEF accordingly, using those three separate subheadings. This is a traditionalist's framework and has the stamp of Michael Gove's legacy, through Nicky Morgan's selection of HMCI Amanda Spielman. Play their game; it is too much of a risk to do otherwise, unless your data is stone-cold excellent – and I truly wish I didn't have to write that. Playing the Ofsted game has never been more important since section 10 inspections ended in 2005. The language you use is important, so write your SEF and construct your arguments carefully, reflecting Ofsted's own language at apposite times. Use the same language during your inspection.

Be aware that quality of education will not get its own section in your report, but it is likely to dominate the writing of it. However, the judgement given for quality of education will very likely limit you to a particular grade – the requires improvement descriptor makes this crystal clear for all key judgements: 'Other than in exceptional circumstances, it is likely that, when the school is judged as requires improvement in any of the key judgements, the school's overall effectiveness will also be requires improvement' (p. 40, S5).

Similarly, if quality of education is judged grade 2, the school cannot be outstanding overall (p. 40, S5).

Intent

Make your intent proud and personal, and make sure that the strapline at least is known to all stakeholders. You have your own circumstances which you have already laid out in the 'context' section, and the intent of your curriculum may thus be different to that of other schools. The section 5 handbook is clear on this (para. 170, p. 41) and your curriculum will be bespoke to your school. What is in your curriculum that is unique to your school? How have you designed your curriculum to reflect this?

Ofsted say, 'Intent is about what leaders intend pupils to learn. It's as simple as that.'[3] But they also add: '"Intent" is not the next big thing.' However, if not *the* big thing, it is certainly one of the biggest, and this

---

3   Heather Fearn, Busting the 'intent' myth, *Ofsted Blog: Schools, Early Years, Further Education and Skills* (1 July 2019). Available at: https://educationinspection.blog.gov.uk/2019/07/01/busting-the-intent-myth.

area of your SEF needs to be written with care. There is, unfortunately, a game to play. The game is in the language.

The new language in the inspection handbook, such as 'intent', 'implementation' and 'impact' (which now has a split meaning for Ofsted), 'research' (mentioned 26 times in this handbook and not once in the previous one), 'cultural capital', 'deep dive', learning as an 'alteration in long-term memory' and the 'substance' of education (yes, amazing isn't it? The substance of education is brand new to the Ofsted lexicon), is all new to this framework. They are all words and phrases to know, and it is worth reflecting them back to your inspectors via your own language in the SEF and on inspection. All inspectors will be trained on this. 'Powerful knowledge' has also raised its head at Ofsted events, as has a 'knowledge curriculum', and Ofsted make reference to 'the best that has been thought and said' in relation to 'cultural capital' (para. 176, p. 42, S5). There is no downside to mentioning that you aspire to do the same in your curriculum intent and finding a couple of examples to back this up. Mention your knowledge of the value of educational research thinking and attach it to something you have done, linking it, if possible, to an improved outcome. There is also nothing wrong with saying you are a research-rich school, a phrase that Ofsted have introduced in the EIF. Research will almost certainly drive some of your work and you will be able to point to that.

Ofsted say that 'inspectors will draw evidence about leaders' curriculum intent principally from discussions with senior and subject leaders' (para. 177, p. 43, S5). In terms of preparation, there is likely to be a much greater burden on middle leaders in subject deep dives. Ensure those leaders are fully briefed on the school's curriculum intent and that it is then sequenced in their own subject to enhance pupils' knowledge. I fully understand the pressures on subject leaders in the foundation subjects in primary schools, especially small ones. The extra work it has caused has been awful for some, but this is Ofsted's doing and it is something that head teachers are going to have to plan for on inspection. In addition, state that you quality assure your curriculum intent through regular meetings – the need for quality assurance of your intent has been stressed to inspectors in EIF training. However, that is all you need to do. Please don't go down the route of getting someone in to help your subject leaders to practise deep dives. And if your local authority, or school improvement partners, say they are going to do this in school reviews, please get together with other primary head teachers and just say no. It is unnecessary and will cause anxiety and extra work.

The most important paragraph when considering how to write the 'intent' section of your SEF is paragraph 172, p. 41, S5, but your context will also drive your curriculum (fourth bullet point of para. 172, p. 41, S5) and Ofsted will be looking for that too. Ofsted say they will 'judge schools taking radically different approaches to the curriculum fairly' (para. 175, p. 42, S5). We will see whether that is true when the first reports come in for Montessori and Steiner schools and some faith schools. For instance, I know of some Jewish schools which devote up to 50% of their timetable to Jewish studies (Kodesh). I hope inspectors see such curricula as containing rich enhancements to the national curriculum and not curriculum narrowing instead (para. 176, p. 42, S5). Time and report judgements will tell here.

Feedback from inspection training shows that inspectors expect to see that intent is monitored and quality assured as part of your curriculum monitoring. Inspectors suggested that, in terms of that monitoring, quality assurance of the curriculum appears to be a frontrunner for the new monitoring of progress. Ignore this at your peril, although it is tough on subject leaders. The focus for curriculum has shifted to subject leaders from senior leaders, who must now ensure that they can evidence the intent of the curriculum in their subject.

Whatever you write, make it proud. Make it the *substance* of your school's education, even if you think the phrase and philosophy is baloney and that the substance of education is something very different from Ofsted's view. Ensure that you describe how your curriculum equips your pupils with 'the knowledge and cultural capital to succeed in life' and give examples of where your curriculum delivers 'the best that has been thought and said', and that you had this firmly in mind when developing your curriculum. Play the game. If you believe in Ofsted's new game, all's well and good, but there are deep reservations among school leaders as to whether this is the game we should be playing. You may be one of them. However, to succeed here, your curriculum intent should be the curriculum intent for which Ofsted are very clearly looking.

Implementation

As well as explaining how you are realising your intent by planning and sequencing your curriculum, this is the place where you say how good your teaching is. No separate judgement is now made about the quality of teaching, but under 'implementation' (p. 51, S5), seven out of ten of the judgement criteria for good mention or infer teaching. The other three criteria are around reading and phonics, so this is where in your SEF you explain how you encourage and plan for both. There is a grade 4 criterion bullet on the same page which avoids mentioning teaching explicitly, but is worth a note: 'The pupils' experiences in lessons contribute weakly to their learning of the intended curriculum' (p. 51, S5).

Within these descriptors, 'knowledge', 'content', 'remember' and, of course, 'curriculum' are mentioned. All these words are sprinkled liberally around this and other areas of the EIF, so reflect that language in your writing.

Within 'implementation', describe your quality of teaching but link it, as the bullet points (para. 183, p. 44, S5) mainly do, to your curriculum and to your published results, or the trends therein.

If you are a school whose results may be on the grade 2/3 borderline, and you don't feel you have had sufficient time to embed an improved curriculum, it is worth knowing that Ofsted may give you some leeway. This will only happen in the first two years of this framework though. Ofsted say: 'Inspectors will bear in mind that developing and embedding an effective curriculum takes time, and that leaders may only be partway through the process of adopting or redeveloping a curriculum' (para. 180, p. 44, S5). This gives you some elbow room, but this does only apply to the implementation of your curriculum, not to intent.

Internal assessment data is something that Ofsted, in their wisdom, have decided they will not take into account on inspection. However, if you are inspected late in the year, your published data may be almost a year out of date. Yes, show how you are improving through your books and your improved curriculum, but that leaves a large degree of subjective judgement. A lead inspector could see what they see and use exactly the same evidence to back their thoughts about grade 2 or grade 3, either in your section 5 or in the letter you will receive if you have a section 8. There is nothing wrong with presenting your internal data to inspectors. You never know what could influence your lead inspector's thinking, and the worst they can do is say they will ignore it, but they can't avoid seeing it! To avoid too much overlap, I have dealt with this difficulty further in Appendix 1. Also use the handbook guidance on the use of internal assessment (paras 185–188, p. 45, S5).

It is well worth digesting paragraph 189 (p. 46, S5). It's about how inspectors will evidence your curriculum implementation. Discussions will be held with subject leaders, teachers, curriculum leaders and pupils. Schemes of work will be reviewed and observations made in class. Inspectors will probe for the depth of subject knowledge that teachers have and any continuing professional development (CPD) offered to support it. The hegemony of subjects is writ bold and subject leaders have become a major focus of inspection teams, with all its workload implications. Your inspection preparation therefore needs to be centred around informing and upskilling all stakeholders in explaining your curriculum intentions and its implementation. Should this include pupils? It's up to you.

For more on how inspectors will go about gathering evidence, on all aspects of the framework, please go to Chapter 3, where I describe the methodology of the EIF from an inspector's point of view.

Impact

Let's start by examining the full section 5 handbook grade descriptor for impact under the heading of 'good quality of education' (p. 51). Most readers will be familiar with the first two bullet points (below). Evidencing academic achievement has become second nature to most leaders in schools, as you have been asked to do it through many frameworks. You are still asked to do it in the EIF, but there are subtle changes:

- Pupils develop detailed knowledge and skills across the curriculum and, as a result, achieve well. This is reflected in results from national tests and examinations that meet government expectations, or in the qualifications obtained.

- Pupils are ready for the next stage of education, employment or training. They have the knowledge and skills they need and, where relevant, they gain qualifications that allow them to go on to destinations that meet their interests and aspirations and the intention of their course of study. Pupils with SEND achieve the best possible outcomes.

- Pupils' work across the curriculum is of good quality.
- Pupils read widely and often, with fluency and comprehension appropriate to their age. They are able to apply mathematical knowledge, concepts and procedures appropriately for their age.

A best-fit approach is used across the four impact grade descriptors, together with the four descriptors for intent and the 10 descriptors for implementation. That is 18 criteria, all subjective, on which to judge quality of education as being good or requires improvement (for the latter, the quality of education has to be simply not good). The final team meeting takes place on day two, when all the inspectors are tired and are working under time pressure, so how much weight is given to individual descriptors, and especially the two descriptors that refer to (just the first) or imply (the second) good published results? In addition, neither descriptor puts pupil progress first and foremost, whereas both contain statements about pupils' attainment.

That is a worry, and the first bullet appears to suggest that, for Ofsted, to 'achieve' now means to 'attain'. I hope not, but there is no definition in the EIF of what achievement means and there are precious few references to achievement, in academic terms, at all. Perhaps the closest reference is under 'Evaluating sixth-form provision in schools', and this provides cold comfort, seemingly substituting 'achievement' for 'attainment' (para. 292, p. 83, S5).

Ofsted would much rather define progress in terms of something different in the EIF, rather than published results, and to be fair, they say that this framework is more about curriculum than it is about a school's league table results. Their new outlook is represented in the statement: 'the progress that pupils are making in terms of knowing more, remembering more and being able to do more' (para. 197, p. 48, S5). How Ofsted will accurately measure any of this progress is a mystery. It has to remain an extremely subjective judgement, made by looking in books and speaking with staff and pupils. That gives you an edge. Make sure you are able to talk about this in terms of your curriculum, and upskill all stakeholders to be able to *say* they have done this – as, of course, all your pupils are certain to have made progress in these areas.

In addition, while being able to talk about progress in terms of knowing more, remembering more and being able to do more, don't stop referring to your pupils' rates of progress, especially if they are accelerating. Also, don't let this prevent you from describing progress across the whole school. Progress is not published progress at Key Stage 2 in your IDSR. Progress starts with the skills pupils bring with them on entry and ends with their attainment when they leave. This must also take into account transience (movement in and out) and outliers – especially caused by the degree of SEND some pupils bring with them. Although contextual value added is not a published measure any more, build a picture of your disadvantage through your 'context' section. No inspector should ignore high levels of disadvantage. Use *anything* that could persuade and eventually convince your lead inspector about your way of thinking. The worst they can do is try to ignore it.

Ofsted will also judge progress in curriculum across the whole school based on deep dives to get a longitudinal view of your curriculum. There is more on these in Chapter 3 about inspection methodology.

Looking back to those impact descriptors, in painting the most convincing picture of the impact of your school's work, use your published data and up-to-date internal data, explaining it with commentary as you go along. Describe how this helps your pupils to be ready for the next stage of their education – or at least, readier than they may have been had they not attended your school. Link this to your curriculum planning and delivery too. Stress your focus on reading and how this is helping pupils to progress.

If you are a primary school or an infant school, include your early years data in this section of your SEF. It sits better here than in your early years section and you can link to other data more easily. My advice in *Taking Control*, that skills on entry to the early years was the most crucial piece of data that any primary school can present to Ofsted, still holds. But its importance overall has been downgraded with the EIF's focus on curriculum. Still, it can be a powerful card to play to put your point of view into the mind of your lead inspector.

From skills on entry, you can demonstrate progress across the whole school. Don't be overgenerous in assessing your children's skills to ensure progress is clear across both nursery and reception. Also, on leaving reception, ensure that assessments of whether children have achieved a good level of development (GLD) are not so positive as to put undue pressure on your measures of progress across Key Stage 1. You are in charge of both assessing skills on entry and assessing GLD. You are also in charge of any baseline assessments you may have done because they are all subjective. You are the main arbiter here. Schools do disagree with local authority moderations; however, don't assess wrongly simply to aggrandise early years progress. It will be clear to inspectors if your pupils are much more capable than you are saying, but it would take a current early years specialist to argue with you on points of early years foundation stage profile assessment, and that is generally not the case. Concentrate on demonstrating the cogency of your curriculum, but drop into the conversation your skills on entry and the rapid progress your children make whenever you can. Ensure this is laid out clearly in your SEF.

Don't create a progression profile through the early years which shows either that children make slow progress in nursery or reception or that they make so much progress that Key Stage 1 appears not to build well on the high numbers of children with GLD. Hopefully, in looking at your curriculum via deep dives, inspectors will see that this is not the case, but your SEF is where you can demonstrate this. I must stress that nothing changes for the pupils. They make the same progress, in the same curriculum, from entry to the end of Key Stage 1, but a lack of cleverness can leave you presenting a weak Key Stage 1, or weaknesses in early years, to your lead inspector, which could create a difficulty and an unnecessary curriculum focus in those areas. All these assessments are in your hands, so be sensible.

Your previous lead inspector's assessment of the children's skills on entry, as described in your last inspection report, can be used as a guide (there is unlikely to be anything of the sort in your report under the new framework).

If you are an infant school, and especially if you have a deprived catchment, then a very careful establishment of the children's skills on entry to your school is vital. Be as conservative as you can with your initial skills assessment. If you have no nursery, you have only three years in which to demonstrate progress and a compelling curriculum to your inspectors. If your exit data is still showing attainment below national norms, the only way to demonstrate progress, beyond leaving it to inspectors to see on deep dives, is by describing academic progress from very low skills on entry to pupils' outcomes in Year 2. In this situation, progress to Key Stage 1 outcomes that are well below national averages can still represent excellent progress, if handled well. Again, use the description of skills on entry from your last inspection report as a guide – and if you can show that these have declined over the intervening period, all the better.

Hopefully, your lead inspector will understand how to determine progress across an infant school, and what they are looking for has changed greatly. In many infant schools, the issue of progress won't now come up; the focus will be on curriculum. But if your lead inspector wants to bring up IDSR information, and your catchment is more deprived than average, they are likely to see poor comparisons to national attainment norms. Thus, if your catchment is disadvantaged, make sure you are able to talk progress from starting points across your school.

I'm including this information on data, even though Ofsted say the focus of inspection will be on curriculum, particularly for schools on the grade 1/2 or grade 2/3 cusp. Already under this framework I have had people complaining to me that whatever they showed inspectors, they appeared to be finding information, via their new methodology, to back the lower of the two grades. It is a continuing worry that inspections are still being shaped by published data, and the influence of this on the mind of the lead inspector varies from inspection to inspection. It is simply not consistent enough. If you are one of those schools, be very wary of trusting your lead inspector to come through your doors with a completely open mind. And, as we've seen, the descriptors for quality of education make it very clear that your published data will still play a part in your inspection via your lead inspector's thinking. Make space in your SEF to explain why your data is what it is. Your lead inspector has to read it. Only ignore my advice here if you are nailed on certain that your data won't cause you a problem.

Let's now have a look at some of the things that can affect progress measures in primary schools and how you may be able to use them to convince an HMI that your progress or attainment may not be quite as they appear in your IDSR.

There are three things that schools can analyse further, and all three could provide a powerful lifeline if your data does not reach what, in your lead inspector's eyes, is an 'acceptable' level. There are no benchmarks, of course.

Possible grade 2 lifelines for a primary school

1. Transience (stability)

Be very clear on how transience, both into and out of your cohort through a key stage, may have affected your data. High transience can be very helpful in explaining why attainment outcomes may not be showing correctly in your IDSR. It therefore has the potential to influence your lead inspector's thinking.

First, be sure on which pupils bring data with them and which don't. This tells you who will be included in your progress score.[4] On page 7 it states:

> Pupils who do not have Key Stage 1 data for all of English reading, English writing and mathematics (for example, those who entered a school from another jurisdiction, or who were absent at the time of the Key Stage 1 assessments), cannot be included in the progress measures, but their Key Stage 2 scores will be included in their school's attainment measures.

There is little in your IDSR or school performance tables to help you with outlining your transience, so you must evidence this yourself using whatever information you can. If transience in your last Year 6/Year 2 cohort was higher than usual, my advice is to disaggregate your transient pupils for your Year 6 (and possibly Year 2) cohorts and recalculate your attainment and progress data without them. Tabulate this alongside your published data. The results could be illuminating – and your inspectors should 'consider' all data presented by you (para. 79, p. 23, S5). However, if it doesn't help you, don't put it in your SEF.

---

4 Your reference document here is: Department for Education, *Primary School Accountability in 2019: A Technical Guide for Primary Maintained Schools, Academies and Free Schools* (December 2019). Available at: https://www.gov.uk/government/publications/primary-school-accountability.

Here is an example to illustrate where the IDSR can be badly wrong. Some years ago, I led the inspection of a primary school which was practically surrounded by an army base. Almost all their pupils were transients as their parents moved often and did tours abroad. The average length of pupils' stay was about two years. The data showed blue across the board (remember the old RAISEonline?), and when I first looked at the school's data it seemed horrendous. All I thought was 'grade 4'. However, you never know what you will find when you walk through the door of a school, and within 10 minutes and finding 95% transience, we effectively took their RAISEonline and placed it in the bin. The school was quite wonderful. What they were doing with the kids, many of whom came from some very challenging backgrounds, was nothing short of remarkable. This was an outstanding school with potentially special measures published data. Your IDSR may not tell the whole story.

It is easy to forget the pupils who left during Key Stage 2. These may have been of high ability or had progressed, in your care, to being pupils who were working at a high level. They would have benefitted your attainment results had they stayed. If you have higher than average transience, I'm sure you have had examples of some very bright pupils who have left to join another school just before their SATs. Don't be afraid to speculate on the attainment you have lost out on due to higher ability pupils leaving late in Key Stage 2. It is all grist to the mill. The same caveat applies: if the results don't benefit you, don't present them to your HMI.

2. Outliers

By outliers, I mean the lowest-performing pupils in your attainment and progress IDSR scatterplots. These pupils are lower and well detached from the main body of pupils on those graphs. The effects of outliers can represent a second possible grade 2 lifeline. Ofsted have taken action in the last couple of years by removing some of the more extreme outliers; however, above a certain level some may still remain. Look at your scatterplots and see if those remaining had a negative effect.

These outliers will all have a story. Pupils underperform for a reason. Present a spreadsheet/annotated copy of your IDSR scatterplot showing each of your outliers and the story behind their lower than expected performance. SEND, English as an additional language (EAL), disadvantage and/or vulnerability are often involved, together with transience, and these factors may overlap. It is important to get down to pupil level on these outliers, as you may be talking about a small number of pupils who are outrageous outliers. In a small primary, especially, this could badly skew your data. Even in a larger primary, the effect of a few extreme outliers can have an inordinate effect on what would have been good progress and attainment data. It may be that your inclusive curriculum benefitted these outliers in very positive ways too.

Jamie Pembroke (@jpembroke on Twitter and very well worth following) highlights another issue with outliers:

> The current KS2 VA [value-added] methodology means outliers are inevitable. The issue centres on pre-key stage pupils and nominal scores. VA estimates for low prior attaining (PA) SEND pupils are too high due to high progress rates of low PA EAL pupils. SEND and EAL pupils with low PA [are] treated the same and have the same benchmarks. The nominal scoring system therefore gives rise to negative VA scores as low as -25 (hopefully, these will have been removed by Ofsted, but the example and calculation remain valid). This makes me mad when accountability guidance states progress measure will reflect progress made by all pupils. Nonsense!
>
> In this example, every other pupil in a class of 25 would have to gain at least +1.0 in their progress measure to compensate for that one extreme outlier. If you had a pupil, in a class of 25, whose progress score was -5, they will have reduced the overall cohort's progress score by 0.2.[5]

It is well worth getting to the bottom of why you have outliers (if indeed you do) and explaining the performance of those particularly low-performing pupils in detail. Know your stuff here. Know it better than your lead inspector. Know it so well that you can teach that lead inspector and be able to link this data to your curriculum – always the best position for a school to be in!

3. Explain the progress of your current pupils fully

To back what I have already said: inspectors are charged not to use internal assessment data. Instead, Ofsted say: 'Inspectors will be

---

5   Personal communication.

interested in the conclusions drawn and actions taken from any internal assessment information, but they will not examine or verify that information first hand' (para. 194, p. 47, S5). But you never know what might influence the person leading your inspection, so include it in your SEF nevertheless, tying recent improvements in different years to curriculum improvements.

You could be showing poor data in your previous IDSR, especially if the leadership team is new. However, curriculum, leadership and teaching could have been already improving, but this may not have had enough time to take full effect by publication time. I hope your inspection team is skilled enough to identify this improvement through deep dives, work scrutinies, interviews or other data collection techniques during your inspection. However, there is nothing wrong with putting your assessment information under the lead inspector's – then other inspectors' – noses via your SEF. Data may not be improving just in the current Year 6 and Year 2, but improvements may be clear in other year groups too, and progress may already have been accelerating in those year groups during the previous year. If you can persuade the team of this, it would augur well for the future and put them in a favourable collective mindset. Set out these legacy issues in your SEF – for example, if the leadership team is new or progress has been historically weak but is now accelerating.

None of this will have been seen in last year's IDSR, of course. Stress these unseen (to your inspectors in the pre-inspection data they are given) progress improvements and clearly explain the links to improving quality curriculum in your SEF. If you can persuade your inspection team that a corner has already been turned in pupil progress, you may have a vital way into persuading your lead inspector that they should be looking at your curriculum in a positive light, to, say, create a convincing evidence base for a grade 2 section 5 outcome or a continuing good section 8 outcome. That initial mindset is very important to you.

4. Other lifelines

All this advice about possible lifelines will enable you and your leaders to talk about the academic progress of your pupils in depth and link it to their progress within the curriculum, if you need to and if you get the chance. Your knowledge about your school will then exceed that of your lead inspector and they can learn from you. That is a comfortable control position to be in. Your lead inspector is human too and his or her work has to fit a framework and Ofsted's report writing expectations. By taking control, you will be able to help them do that.

Your lead inspector has to ensure they can get their grade through quality assurance. As a consequence, they will work with you to show your school in the best possible light *only* if they need to get your data to fit their projected higher grade. If the inspector is on your side and the team believe you are a good school, but there is information that doesn't, on the surface, support a grade of good, they will shape what they see so that it reflects the good criteria in the handbook. This could involve being influenced by the three lifeline possibilities discussed in this section, and working with you to ensure that the finished quality of education evidence fits the quality of education criteria. However, if your HMI becomes convinced you are a grade 3 or grade 4 school, they will still be working to get your data to fit their grade – but that won't be a help to you. Remember: every decision made by your lead inspector and the inspection team is subjective. Glass half-full or glass half-empty? Help your lead inspector to decide! Be prepared via your SEF and don't leave your outcome completely to chance on the day.

Junior schools and middle schools

Together with other institutions like studio schools and university technical colleges, junior and middle schools are examples of schools that start and stop at non-standard ages. Ofsted say they take into account national expectations differently in such schools:

> Pupils at junior schools, on average, have higher attainment scores at the end of key stage 2 than pupils at all other primary schools. However, on average, they also have lower progress scores. This may be for a variety of reasons, and inspectors will take this into account when comparing their results with those of pupils in schools that start education from the beginning of key stage 1. (para. 308, p. 90, S5)

If you are a junior school, then this framework could be a blessing. At last, you won't be saddled with Key Stage 1 data over which you have no control. You will be inspected around your own curriculum and the progress that your pupils make within it. However, the problems with your inherited Key Stage 1 data and progress still remain. It's clear that Ofsted are aware of this problem from the wording in the extract above. At least the word 'will' appears in the paragraph. Inspectors therefore have to take your possible data difficulties into account. Play on this. You have fairly free rein to explain why your progress data is as it is. Use this in your SEF.

For Ofsted, progress across your school is represented by the Key Stage 2 IDSR; your HMI will see no other measure of progress for your school prior to receiving your SEF. Your on-entry data is the exit data from your infant school(s), and if I were an infant school head teacher I would want to make damn sure that my teacher assessments at Key Stage 1 showed my school in the best possible light.

Why have previous local authority education regimes and governments allowed this infant/junior division to perpetuate? I have supported several sets of infant and junior schools that are separated only by a wall – and in one case, a shared school field – who were so far apart on the assessment of their pupils that they could almost be in different continents. So, which data does an inspector believe? EIF 2019 swings the pendulum back towards junior schools, as it instructs inspectors to take account of the fact that, nationally, Key Stage 2 published progress in junior schools is slower than in primary schools.

If you are a junior or an infant school, follow the advice contained in this book and fight your own corner. I know of instances where separate, two-form entry infant and junior schools have been judged to be good because both were very persuasive about their data to their respective and different inspection teams, yet overall data from reception to Year 6 might have put a combined school as no better than requires improvement. Crazy but true. With the focus on curriculum this may no longer be the case, so watch out. Battle to convince the inspectors about *your* school. The infant school on the other side of the wall is not being inspected with you.

As a result, junior schools should consider re-basing their on-entry data, perhaps using testing, such as National Foundation for Educational Research (NFER) tests, to determine their own baseline for

Year 3 pupils joining their school. If you don't do this and you accept the on-entry IDSR as correct, your pupils may have to make super-human progress to appear to get even to the national progress norm of 0.0. There is unfairness in this system that often can only be resolved by school amalgamation. Any junior school or infant head teacher who reads this will understand.

A junior school should present re-baselined data alongside its IDSR, then build a persuasive supporting argument via:

■ The evidence you have seen of pupils' starting points in their early work in Year 3 books.

■ The progress you see overall in individual year groups.

■ The progress you see in the books of pupils in all other year groups.

■ An examination of transience and its effect on IDSR outcomes.

■ An explanation of any outliers.

Hopefully this will be recognised both in deep dives and in discussions. In addition, do the same analyses around transient pupils and outliers, as detailed above.

Effectively, if you feel your feeder infant schools over-assess your pupils at the end of Year 2, you have to make the case that IDSR progress scores may well be skewed negatively by that data. You can do this through data in your SEF, but also through the curriculum progress seen in evidence gathering on inspection. Show that your IDSR does not paint an accurate picture of progress in your school and that the progress data is therefore wrong. Experience tells me that this is an argument you can win.

If you are a middle school, again, this framework could be a boon to you – if your curriculum prepares your pupils well for entry into secondary school. Positive evidence from your pupils' destinations, that they have come to them well-prepared, would be very useful here. Your arguments to your inspectors are similar to those of junior schools, but you mustn't let Year 6 IDSR outcome data dominate your inspection. I doubt they will, but be prepared to point inspectors to the following paragraph if, for some reason, that happens:

Pupils at middle schools, on average, have lower progress scores at the end of key stage 2 than pupils at primary schools. Due to the age range of pupils at middle schools, pupils will have only attended a middle school for a short time before they take their key stage 2 tests and will still have a number of years left at the school. Inspectors will take this into account when comparing pupils' results to those of schools that start educating their pupils from the beginning of key stage 1. (para. 309, pp. 90–91, S5)

Nail your attainment on entry, first and foremost. Baseline your pupils carefully and evidence their attainment when they leave just as thoroughly. Use your own or other commercial products to measure pupil progress across your school, attainment when they leave and their progress within year groups. Remember, inspectors must look at all the evidence presented to them. Show inspectors how well your pupils progress in your curriculum during the time they are there and that your curriculum is well-sequenced from Key Stage 2 to Key Stage 3.

Prepare your data arguments well, but consider your unique position with regard to your curriculum straddling Key Stage 2/3 and pupils not leaving at the end of a publicly reported key stage as a big, positive lever to your inspection grade.

Early years

Early years are given a separate judgement grade on inspection and bespoke judgement criteria. Thus, there is a discrete section in the handbook devoted to evaluating the quality of early years education (paras 279–289, pp. 77–82, S5).

There are particular factors that inspectors should take into account in early years (para. 282, p. 77, S5):

■ the extent to which leaders and staff plan, design and implement the curriculum

- the extent to which the curriculum and care practices meet the needs of the range of children who attend, particularly any children with SEND

- the progress all children make in their learning and development relative to their starting points and their readiness for the next stage of their education[6]

- children's personal, social and emotional development, including whether they feel safe and are secure, stimulated and happy.

Although it is graded, early years no longer gets a separate section in the report. There is usually a short paragraph reporting what inspectors have found, but not always, despite the length of the descriptors. Two words jump out from the descriptors around curriculum and academic intentions. The first is 'ambitious' and the second is 'reading', so reflect both of these focuses in your writing.

All the other major inspection areas are also inspected in early years: the quality of education, behaviour and attitudes, personal development, and leadership and management. Numerical grades are not given for each separate area in a section 5 inspection; instead, grades will be implicit, or even explicit, in the report. For example, this kind of phrase may be used as an opener, 'Leaders in the early years reflect the high standards and expectations seen across the whole school,' and then each separate area will be included in subsequent bullet points.

In your SEF, set out early years as a series of subheadings, with an initial context statement and a short paragraph for each of the major areas that will be inspected. Mirror the separate sections in your main school SEF. Apply all the advice contained in the separate self-evaluation chapters. When writing your 'quality of education' section, however, don't repeat all of the data contained in your main school 'quality of education' section. Instead, refer briefly to this information and repeat your overall conclusions about the entry, exit and progress data of children in early years.

---

6   Even though inspectors are expected to 'get beyond the data as quickly as possible to ascertain how well the curriculum is meeting children's needs' (para. 284, p. 77, S5), this means that a data conversation can certainly take place. This will give you an opportunity to take control and explain how well your children are doing from the starting points you have determined. That is quite an opportunity and quite a lever!

2.3. Secondary Self-Evaluation

You can find the secondary self-evaluation dialogic tool in Appendix 2. Use that tool, in conjunction with the advice in this chapter, to write your self-evaluation. While writing, have the Ofsted handbook with you and quote from it, where necessary, to illustrate the evidence for your grade judgement. I won't reiterate all that is in the secondary SEF tool guidance here, but I will refer to the relevant sections.

Here is a summary of what you should include in the first section of your SEF:

■ Set out your grade stall (e.g. 'We believe we are a good school') right from the start. Be clear on this and use the rest of the SEF to support this statement.

■ Set your school in an Ofsted grade context and then in your local context. Provide evidence of how you have translated your vision to all leaders and staff here (see section 2.6 for more on this).

■ Provide information about your school using your last inspection report as your template. The 'information about your school' section no longer appears in the EIF, but it is worth using this subheading to give your inspectors a fuller idea of your school.

■ Show how you have met the key issues from your previous inspection.

Following this introductory part, there is no doubt that the most important section of your SEF is the 'quality of education' section. I will provide advice around other sections when we join up with the primary narrative, so I will concentrate on quality of education here. As we saw in Chapter 1, curriculum is now king but data is the joker in the pack, and I will offer plenty of tips on how you can use both to best effect.

The sixth form is evaluated separately and given a grade. As the data here does not overlap or continue in a linear way from GCSE data, the sixth-form data can sit in your '16–19' section and not your 'quality of education' section.

Quality of education

There are big changes here from the previous framework. Much of your work will be assessed by looking at the cogency of your curriculum from Year 7 to Year 11. Make no mistake, Ofsted are looking for a particular approach with regard to curriculum intent and implementation – impact remains similar – so organise your SEF accordingly. This is a traditionalist's framework and has the stamp of Michael Gove's legacy – through Nicky Morgan's selection of HMCI Amanda Spielman – throughout. Play their game; it is too much of a risk to do otherwise, unless your data is stone-cold excellent – and I truly wish I didn't have to write that. Playing the Ofsted game has never been more important since section 10 inspections ended in 2005. The language you use is important, so write your SEF and construct your arguments carefully, reflecting Ofsted's own language at apposite times. Use the same language during your inspection.

Be aware that quality of education will not get its own section in your report, but it is likely to dominate the writing of it. However, the judgement given for quality of education will very likely limit you to grade 2 – the requires improvement descriptor makes this clear for all key judgements: 'Other than in exceptional circumstances, it is likely that, when the school is judged as requires improvement in any of the key judgements, the school's overall effectiveness will also be requires improvement' (p. 40, S5).

Similarly, if quality of education is judged grade 2, the school cannot be outstanding overall (p. 40, S5).

Judgement and context

Begin with your own judgement, then include a short context paragraph summarising your thinking and matching the content to your grade.

Intent

Make your intent proud and personal, and make sure that the strapline at least is known to all stakeholders. You have your own circumstances which you have already laid out in the 'context' section, and the intent of your curriculum may thus be different to that of other schools. The section 5 handbook is clear on this (para. 170, p. 41) and your curriculum will be bespoke to your school. What is in your curriculum that is unique to your school? How have you designed your curriculum to reflect this?

Ofsted state, 'Intent is about what leaders intend pupils to learn. It's as simple as that.'[7] But they also add: '"Intent" is not the next big thing.' However, if not *the* big thing, it is certainly one of the biggest, and this area of your SEF needs to be written with care. There is, unfortunately, a game to play. The game is in the language.

The new language in the inspection handbook, such as 'intent', 'implementation' and 'impact' (which now has a split meaning for Ofsted), 'research' (mentioned 26 times in this handbook and not once in the previous one), 'cultural capital', 'deep dive', learning as an 'alteration in long-term memory' and the 'substance' of education (yes, amazing isn't it? The substance of education is brand new to the Ofsted lexicon), is all new to this framework. They are all words and phrases to know, and it is worth reflecting them back to your inspectors via your own language in the SEF and on inspection. All inspectors will be trained on this. 'Powerful knowledge' has also raised its head at Ofsted events, as has a 'knowledge curriculum', and Ofsted make reference to 'the best that has been thought and said' in relation to 'cultural capital' (para. 176, p. 42, S5). There is no downside to mentioning that you aspire to do the same in your curriculum intent and finding a couple of examples to back this up. Mention your knowledge of the value of educational research thinking and attach it to something you have done, linking it, if possible, to an improved outcome. There is also nothing wrong with saying you are a research-rich school, a phrase that Ofsted have introduced in the EIF. Research will almost certainly drive some of your work and you will be able to point to that.

Ofsted say that 'inspectors will draw evidence about leaders' curriculum intent principally from discussions with senior and subject leaders' (para. 177, p. 43, S5). In terms of preparation, there is likely to be a much greater burden on middle leaders in subject deep dives. Ensure those leaders are fully briefed on the school's curriculum intent and that

---

7   Heather Fearn, Busting the 'intent' myth, *Ofsted Blog: Schools, Early Years, Further Education and Skills* (1 July 2019). Available at: https://educationinspection.blog.gov.uk/2019/07/01/busting-the-intent-myth.

it is then sequenced in their own subject to enhance pupils' knowledge. I fully understand the pressures on subject leaders in the foundation subjects in secondary schools. The extra work it has caused has been awful for some, but this is Ofsted's doing and it is something that head teachers are going to have to plan for on inspection. In addition, state that you quality assure your curriculum intent through regular meetings – the need for quality assurance of your intent has been stressed to inspectors in EIF training. However, that is all you need to do. Please don't go down the route of getting someone in to help your subject leaders to practise deep dives. And if your local authority, or school improvement partners, say they are going to do this in school reviews, please get together with other secondary head teachers and just say no. It is unnecessary and will cause anxiety and extra work.

The most important paragraph is para. 172, p. 41, S5 when considering how to write the 'intent' section of your SEF, but your context will also drive your curriculum (fourth bullet point of para. 172, p. 41, S5) and Ofsted will be looking for that too. Feedback from inspection training shows that inspectors expect to see that intent is monitored and quality assured as a part of your curriculum monitoring. Inspectors suggested that, in terms of that monitoring, quality assurance of the curriculum appears to be a frontrunner for the new monitoring of progress. Ignore this at your peril, although it is tough on subject leaders. The focus for curriculum has shifted to subject leaders from senior leaders, who must now ensure that they can evidence the intent of the curriculum in their subject.

Ofsted say they will 'judge schools taking radically different approaches to the curriculum fairly' (para. 175, p. 42, S5). We will see whether that is true when the first reports come in for Montessori and Steiner schools and some faith schools. For instance, I know of some Jewish schools which devote up to 50% of their timetable to Jewish studies (Kodesh). I hope inspectors see such curricula as containing rich enhancements to the national curriculum and not curriculum narrowing (para. 176, p. 42, S5) instead. Time and report judgements will tell here.

In this section, say that you are designing your curriculum with the EBacc in mind and that you intend to work towards the government's expectation that 75% of your GCSE pupils will study EBacc subjects by 2022 (taking exams in 2024), rising to 90% by 2025 (taking exams in 2027).[8] Ofsted do say that 'Inspectors will not make a judgement about the quality of education based solely or primarily on its progress towards the EBacc ambition' (para. 177, p. 43, S5), which gives you plenty of leeway in your writing. If you are a university technical college or a studio school, the government's EBacc ambition does not apply to you. The handbook is very clear on this (paras 310–311, p. 91, S5).

Whatever you write, make it proud. Make it the *substance* of your school's education, even if you think the phrase and philosophy is baloney and that the substance of education is something very different from Ofsted's view. Ensure that you describe how your curriculum equips your pupils with 'the knowledge and cultural capital to succeed in life' and give examples of where your curriculum delivers 'the best that has been thought and said', and that you had this firmly in mind when developing your curriculum. Play the game. If you believe in Ofsted's new game, all is well and good, but there are deep reservations among school leaders as to whether this is the game we should be playing. You may be one of them. However, to succeed here, your curriculum intent should be the curriculum intent that is very clearly being looked for by Ofsted.

Implementation

As well as explaining how you are realising your intent by planning and sequencing your curriculum, this is the place where you say how good your teaching is. No separate judgement is now made about the quality of teaching, but under 'implementation' (p. 51, S5), seven out of ten of the judgement criteria for good mention or infer teaching. The other three criteria are around reading and phonics. Phonics doesn't concern you, but this is where in your SEF you should explain how you encourage and plan for reading. There is a grade 4 criterion bullet on the same page which avoids mentioning teaching explicitly, but is worth a note: 'The pupils' experiences in lessons contribute weakly to their learning of the intended curriculum' (p. 51, S5).

Within these descriptors, 'knowledge', 'content', 'remember' and, of course, 'curriculum' are mentioned. All these words are sprinkled

---

8   See https://www.gov.uk/government/publications/english-baccalaureate-ebacc/english-baccalaureate-ebacc.

liberally around this and other areas of the EIF, so reflect that language in your writing.

Under 'implementation', describe your quality of teaching but link it, as the bullet points mainly do (para. 183, p. 44, S5), to your curriculum and to your published results, or the trends therein.

If you are a school whose results may be on the grade 2/3 borderline, and you don't feel you have had sufficient time to embed an improved curriculum, it is worth knowing that Ofsted may give you some leeway. This will only happen in the first two years of this framework though. Ofsted say: 'Inspectors will bear in mind that developing and embedding an effective curriculum takes time, and that leaders may only be partway through the process of adopting or redeveloping a curriculum' (para. 180, p. 44, S5). This gives you some elbow room, but this does only apply to the implementation of your curriculum, not to intent.

Internal assessment data is something that Ofsted, in their wisdom, have decided they will not take into account on inspection. However, if you are inspected late in the year, your published data may be almost a year out of date. Yes, show how you are improving through your books and your improved curriculum, but that leaves a large degree of subjective judgement. A lead inspector could see what they see and use exactly the same evidence to back their thoughts about grade 2 or grade 3, either in your section 5 or in the letter you will receive if you have a section 8. There is nothing wrong with presenting your internal data to inspectors. You never know what could influence your lead inspector's thinking, and the worst they can do is say they will ignore it, but they can't avoid seeing it! To avoid too much overlap, I have dealt with this difficulty further in Appendix 2. Also refer to the handbook guidance on the use of internal assessment (paras 185–188, p. 45, S5).

Paragraph 189 (p. 46, S5) is well worth digesting. It is about how inspectors will evidence your curriculum implementation. Discussions will be held with subject leaders, teachers, curriculum leaders and pupils. Schemes of work will be reviewed and observations made in class. Inspectors will probe for the depth of subject knowledge that teachers have and any continuing professional development (CPD) offered to support it. The hegemony of subjects is writ bold and subject leaders have become a major focus of inspection teams, with all its workload implications. Your inspection preparation, therefore, needs to be centred around informing and upskilling all stakeholders in explaining your curriculum intentions and its implementation. Should this include pupils? It's up to you.

For more on how inspectors will go about gathering evidence, on all aspects of the framework, please go to Chapter 3, where I describe the methodology of the EIF from an inspector's point of view.

Impact

With luck, you won't need this section on inspection, but you might. The focus will be on curriculum via deep dives. Many secondary schools are reporting no conversations around data, either at senior or subject leader level. This section is not so much about what happens during inspection, but more about persuading your lead inspector that you are the school you say you are. However, two bullets in the grade descriptor for impact (see below) refer to published data or the qualifications that pupils gain when they leave. Your data still counts in that assessment of your grade and, as I will argue, it may well have a greater weight than would seem to be the case in the minds of some lead inspectors.

Let's start by examining the full section 5 handbook grade descriptor for impact under the heading of 'good quality of education' (p. 51). Most readers will be familiar with the first two bullets (below). Evidencing academic achievement has become second nature to most leaders in schools, as you have been asked to do it through many frameworks. You are still asked to do it in the EIF, but there are subtle changes:

- Pupils develop detailed knowledge and skills across the curriculum and, as a result, achieve well. This is reflected in results from national tests and examinations that meet government expectations, or in the qualifications obtained.

- Pupils are ready for the next stage of education, employment or training. They have the knowledge and skills they need and, where relevant, they gain qualifications that allow them to go on to destinations that meet their interests and aspirations and the intention of their course of study. Pupils with SEND achieve the best possible outcomes.

- Pupils' work across the curriculum is of good quality.

> ■ Pupils read widely and often, with fluency and comprehension appropriate to their age. They are able to apply mathematical knowledge, concepts and procedures appropriately for their age.

A best-fit approach is used across the four impact grade descriptors, together with the four descriptors for intent and the 10 descriptors for implementation. That is 18 criteria, all subjective, on which to judge quality of education as being good or requires improvement (for the latter, the quality of education has to be simply not good). The final team meeting takes place on day two, when all the inspectors are tired and are working under time pressure, so how much weight is given to individual descriptors, and especially the two descriptors that refer to (just the first) or imply (the second) good published results? In addition, neither descriptor puts pupil progress first and foremost, whereas both contain statements about pupils' attainment. However, the following from 'Evaluating sixth-form provision in schools' appears to muddy the waters, creating a possible confusion between achievement and attainment: 'the extent to which leaders and teachers have high expectations for achievement and progress' (para. 292, p. 83, S5).

Ofsted would much rather define progress in terms of something different in the EIF, rather than published results, and to be fair, they say that this framework is more about curriculum than it is about a school's league table results. This is more their new outlook: 'the progress that pupils are making in terms of knowing more, remembering more and being able to do more' (para. 197, p. 48, S5).

How Ofsted will accurately measure any of this progress is a mystery. It has to remain an extremely subjective judgement, made by looking in books and speaking with staff and pupils. That gives you an edge. Make sure you are able to talk about this in terms of your curriculum, and upskill all stakeholders to be able to *say* they have done this – as, of course, all your pupils are certain to have made progress in these areas. In addition, while being able to talk about progress in terms of knowing more, remembering more and being able to do more, don't stop referring to your pupils' rates of progress, especially if they are accelerating.

Progress 8 (the Department for Education's measure of progress in secondary schools) compares pupils' skills on entry to their attainment when they leave. This must also take into account transience (movement in and out) and outliers – especially caused by the degree of SEND some pupils bring with them. Although contextual value added is not a published measure any more, build a picture of your disadvantage through your 'context' section. No inspector should ignore high levels of disadvantage. Use *anything* that could persuade and eventually convince your lead inspector about your way of thinking. The worst they can do is try to ignore it.

Ofsted will also judge progress in curriculum across the whole school based on deep dives to get a longitudinal view of your curriculum. There is more on these in Chapter 3 about inspection methodology.

Looking back to those impact descriptors, in painting the most convincing picture of the impact of your school's work, use your published data and up-to-date internal data, explaining it with commentary as you go along. Describe how this helps your pupils to be ready for the next stage of their education – or at least, readier than they may have been had they not attended your school. Link this to your curriculum planning and delivery too. Stress your focus on reading and how this is helping pupils to progress. If your NEETs (not in education, employment or training) are fewer than the national average, this can be very good data to show that your curriculum is suiting your pupils very well.

We must remember that curriculum is king but data, the joker in the pack, is still playing a part in inspections. With that in mind, let's look at how your data could be used to back an assertion that despite, at face value, less than perfect IDSR/Analyse School Performance (ASP) data, pupils in your school are still making good progress.

Before we do this, let me state again that I can't save you if your school is not doing a good enough job for your pupils and they really aren't making expected progress. In that case, grade 3 or grade 4 will be a deserved inspection outcome, as may be the consequences. Above everything else – and we may not like this – apart from the expectation that pupils are kept safe, inspection cannot divorce itself from league table data. There is a demand that a good school has good published results, no matter what we may feel about the education of the whole child.

Next, I will describe some possible lifelines if your IDSR and especially your Progress 8 doesn't look great. It has to be said though that there is less wriggle room around data at secondary than at primary level.

Still, here are some possibilities you might be able to play with. Again, if your inspection goes well, it will be curriculum that is the focus. If the result is requires improvement, you will find references to your pupils not doing as well as they could in subjects, and part of that thinking will have been around data.

Possible grade 2 lifelines for a secondary school

1. Is your attainment on entry to Year 7 accurate?

It is possible to argue that assessment by your feeder primaries is inaccurate. Primaries often do a brilliant job in preparing their pupils well for SATs. The pupils reach peak exam performance for those SATs in May of Year 6, but the results achieved may not reflect the actual abilities of pupils. To some extent, they may actually reflect excellent preparation by their teachers for their pupils' SATs. This can be especially true in writing, where primary assessment is by teachers and not via a standardised test. But even in mathematics and reading, pupils may have been very well coached, even tutored, to pass their SATs. (Do you know what proportion of your intake were tutored through their SATs and what impact this had on their results?) Approaches will also differ between your feeder primary schools, so their SATs results may not properly represent pupils' abilities in the subject. Thus, SAT-readiness may not reflect pupils' true abilities at the age of 11.

The Year 7 'dip' is well-documented, but the achievement of pupils prior to the dip can create a false starting point for particular pupils and put your early Key Stage 3 progress results under pressure, if not your progress measures across the whole school. Your inspectors may consider that five years is long enough for you to have redressed any potential over-assessment or targeted SATs exam preparation, but that does not change the fact that it may be there in your prior attainment data and therefore your Year 11 Progress 8 data. If necessary, argue your case that on-entry data for your school may not be as accurate as it could be.

Effectively, if you feel your feeder primary schools over-assess pupils at the end of Key Stage 2, you have to make the case that your Progress 8 progress scores may well be skewed negatively by the data and therefore your IDSR does not paint an accurate picture of progress in your school.

2. Explain the progress of your current pupils fully

3. Explain the progress of pupils in all years fully

I will deal with these two points together. As I have already said, Ofsted state they will not use internal assessment data as evidence, but if it's in your SEF, your lead inspector can't help but see it – and you never know what influence very positive internal assessment data containing lots of very visible greens may do. (Never underestimate the effect in tables of greens and reds on an Ofsted inspector!) If you can get them thinking, 'If this is right, these kids could do very well in a few years' time,' all well and good. There is nothing wrong with dropping into your phone call that you are seeing a real acceleration in progress at Key Stage 3 due to the galvanising effect of your new curriculum. The worst your lead inspector can do is say they must ignore it, but they will be looking for just that in their deep dives. They also will be interested in how your internal assessment information helps you to plan (para. 194, p. 47, S5).

4. Transience (stability)

Be very clear on how transience, both into and out of a cohort, may have affected your GCSE data. A strong explanation of your (possibly) high transience can be another key to explaining why attainment outcomes may not be showing correctly in your IDSR. It may just provide you with a grade 2 lifeline.

Also, be sure about which pupils bring data with them and which don't. If a pupil joins in Year 11 but completed Years 7–10 at a different school (which may not be their only secondary school, of course) their Key Stage 2 data follows them. Thus, progress is calculated to GCSE from Year 7 as if they had been with you. This seriously affects the Progress 8 of university technical colleges (UTCs) and studio schools, none of whose pupils started with them. The section 5 handbook says (para. 311, p. 91, S5):

The progress 8 accountability measure is not the most appropriate performance indicator for UTCs and studio schools. These establishments typically start educating pupils at age 14 and have a focus on preparing pupils for their future careers. Inspectors will pay attention to other measures, particularly pupils' destinations when they leave the UTC or studio school.

In consequence, you can argue that any pupils who join from other schools could be treated in the same way and can be disaggregated from your results. Of course, if the pupils who join are all higher performing and carry on that high performance with you, it's worth quietly burying this information and celebrating their achievements!

In reality, such pupils often have stories, and if a large proportion of them are pupil premium/SEND and have been poor attenders before coming to you, then you could end up responsible for a negative progress outlier that could skew your results. This is especially true for smaller secondaries.

Your transients may well have made good progress in the short time they have been in your care, but they have not had the full experience of your school and you cannot be responsible for a pupil's poor progress in another school. The secondary accountability measures are worth a read here. The Department for Education say: 'We now limit how negative a pupil's progress score can be when calculating the school average.'[9] It still doesn't completely remove the outliers, but at least it is a little fairer.

The same document also states that the Department for Education remove those pupils from Progress 8 measures who have no Key Stage 2 scores (such as those arriving from abroad or from the independent sector). Unless they have recently come from abroad, however, and you ask for them to be removed, they will count in your Attainment 8 measure.

Don't forget the pupils who left during Key Stage 3/4. These pupils may have been, on average, of higher ability than the cohort left behind and may have benefitted your attainment results had they stayed and achieved the average progress of the rest of that cohort. This can be the case if your school is in a catchment with a grammar or private school close by and parents move their pupils for GCSEs. If this is the case, it should be explained carefully in your SEF.

---

9   Department for Education, *Secondary Accountability Measures: Guide for Maintained Secondary Schools, Academies and Free Schools* (October 2019), p. 19. Available at: https://www.gov.uk/government/publications/progress-8-school-performance-measure.

5. Outliers

By outliers, I mean the lowest-performing pupils in your attainment and progress IDSR scatterplots. These pupils are lower and well detached from the main body of pupils on those graphs. The effects of outliers can represent a fifth possible grade 2 lifeline. I have begun to allude to this above. I hope your lead inspector understands the effect that outliers – which could lie beyond your control – may have on your progress and attainment data. If they don't, you must be able to explain.

These outliers will all have a story. Pupils underperform for reasons. Present a spreadsheet showing each of your outlier pupils and the story behind their lower than expected performance. SEND, English as an additional language (EAL), disadvantage and/or vulnerability are often involved, together with transience, and these factors often overlap. It is important to get down to pupil level on these outliers, as you may be talking about a small number of pupils who are outrageous outliers. In a small secondary, especially, this could badly skew your data.

All this advice about possible lifelines will enable you and your leaders to talk about the progress of your pupils in depth, if you need to, but it may well be that data is never mentioned during the inspection. Pre-inspection is when your lead inspector will look at this, to gain an initial feel about the school, so your phone call and then your SEF are the places where you can subtly persuade them that you are doing a good job, before they step across your threshold.

Remember: every decision made by your lead inspector and the inspection team is subjective. It is better to have the lead inspector approaching your school with a mindset that reflects a glass half-full rather than a glass half-empty inspection. It is possible to engineer the best scenario for your school via a cogent and persuasive self-evaluation.

Evaluating sixth-form provision in schools

If you have a sixth form, it is given a separate overall grade on inspection which has discrete judgement criteria. A separate section in the section 5 handbook is devoted to this (paras 290–295, pp. 83–86, S5). All the major areas of school inspection are evaluated during the inspection of the sixth form and the inspection methodology is the same as for the main school. Inspectors will examine the quality of education, the students' behaviour and attitudes and their personal development, together with leadership and management. Numerical grades are not given for each separate area if it is a section 5 inspection; instead, grades will be implicit, or even explicit, in the report.

In your self-evaluation, outline the effectiveness of the sixth form as a series of subheadings for each of the major areas that will be inspected. Apply all the advice contained in the self-evaluation chapters of this book. Sixth-form student outcomes data is specific, however, and doesn't link easily to Year 7–11 data, so it should be included here and not in the 'quality of education' section of your main SEF.

Be prepared and take control via your self-evaluation, especially around quality of education. Don't leave your inspection outcome to chance on the day.

I will now merge my two separated strands of primary and secondary SEF guidance into one narrative. From now on, I will use instances from both phases. Please skip any examples which don't apply to your phase of school.

2.4. Behaviour and Attitudes

The first two paragraphs of the behaviour and attitudes section of the handbook (paras 201–202, pp. 52–53, S5) set out what you must include in this section.

Judgement and context

Begin with making your own judgement, then include a short context paragraph summarising your thinking and match your writing to your grade.

Behaviour and attitudes

Use each of the bullet points (para. 202, pp. 52–53, S5) in your writing. I would advocate using subheadings for each one as this will help you to focus. Ofsted say that they believe all these points are important and are based on research (para. 203, p. 52, S5), so don't miss them out. Combining several under one heading would be fine.

Use your SEF to give pointers to your inspectors as to where they will see good (or better) behaviour and attitudes around your school, but be careful not to just describe your provision. Always link provision to improving outcomes (explain the impact of what you have done in terms of what pupils have learned about behaviour and attitudes through your curriculum) and to academic outcomes, if pupils' behaviour and attitudes have improved and you can evidence this. Also link behaviour and attitudes to teaching and to the impact of leaders' vision, intervention and initiatives. Use numerical data wherever you can. At least the word 'impeccable' has been removed from this framework for attaining a grade of outstanding!

There is specific data you can include, like attendance and exclusion data and data from other school logs, but also use pupil and parent surveys here and comments from other sources that speak favourably about the behaviour and attitudes of your pupils and corroborate your views.

Be aware that behaviour and attitudes will not get its own section in your report – it will get a short paragraph, or two, at best. However, the judgement given for behaviour and attitudes will very likely limit you to grade 2 – the requires improvement descriptor makes this clear for all key judgements: 'Other than in exceptional circumstances, it is likely that, when the school is judged as requires improvement in any of the key judgements, the school's overall effectiveness will also be requires improvement' (p. 40, S5). Similarly, if behaviour and attitudes is judged as grade 2, only in 'exceptional circumstances' could the school be outstanding overall (p. 40, S5).

Ofsted recognise that the school may be working with pupils with particular needs to improve their behaviour or attitudes. In these cases, 'demonstrable improvement' will satisfy the inspection team (para. 204,

p. 53, S5), so include a couple of examples of where previously very challenging pupils have made such improvements.

Feeling safe/bullying

Feeling safe/bullying is an important part of behaviour and attitudes and can severely limit your judgement to inadequate. It will almost certainly have spill-overs into safeguarding too. Explain that your pupils say they feel safe; if you have good questionnaire evidence for this, don't be afraid to repeat a good percentage figure several times in your SEF, including here. This is a limiting judgement for inadequate (inadequate grade descriptor for behaviour and attitudes, pp. 57–58, S5):

- Incidents of bullying or prejudiced and discriminatory behaviour, both direct and indirect, are frequent.

- Pupils have little confidence in the school's ability to tackle harassment, bullying, violence and/or discriminatory behaviour successfully.

- Pupils or particular groups of pupils are not safe or do not feel safe at school and/or at alternative placements.

Behaviour and attitudes both overlap into safeguarding, which is covered in section 2.6 on leadership and management. You should site your main writing about safeguarding under leadership and management, but a mention here about safeguarding quality, specifically around feeling safe, would be sensible.

Attendance and punctuality

The section on attendance and punctuality is the place to include your attendance information as well as anything you have on punctuality. Show patterns of improving attendance over time, if you can, especially of persistent absentees. Attendance can be a limiting judgement for inadequate when it comes to behaviour and attitudes, and could therefore lead to inadequate for overall effectiveness. This is when attendance is extremely low and has been over time: 'Attendance is consistently low for all pupils or groups of pupils and shows little sign of sustained improvement' (inadequate grade descriptor for behaviour and attitudes, p. 57, S5).

That seems scary, but I have never seen a school hanged simply on attendance. Neither did I hang a school or was on a team that hung a school on attendance either when I was inspecting. If a school is clearly good overall in every other respect, but attendance has been a historical bugbear, I have found ways around it, sometimes with my quality assurance reader's support, to write attendance to somehow fit the good descriptors.

Ofsted will visit or call any off-site unit that the school runs for pupils whose behaviour is poor or have low attendance (para. 231, p. 55, S5). More information about off-site provision can be found in the section on 'inspecting off-site provision' (paras 247–253, pp. 67–68, S5).

Coronavirus update

School closures during the COVID-19 outbreak have thrown an enormous spanner into the works of school attendance data. We will need to see how this pans out, but be prepared to argue your case robustly that you cared for all your pupils, supporting them at home, or in school, very well through this time.

Exclusion

There is an increased focus on exclusion in the EIF, as well as off-rolling (discussed in section 2.6). So, explain your figures carefully, highlighting any improvements over time which relate to both permanent and fixed-term exclusions. Ensure you can evidence that permanent exclusions are always a last resort. Inspectors are expected to gather evidence on this (paras 206–208, p. 53, S5; para. 213, p. 55, S5).

2.5. Personal Development (including Spiritual, Moral, Social and Cultural Development)

In this handbook, 'personal development' gets its own section (paras 216–218, pp. 58–59, S5), distinct from the old 'personal development, behaviour and welfare' in the previous framework.

Be aware that personal development will not get its own section in your report. It will get a short paragraph, at best, with elements of personal development possibly scattered through other paragraphs. However, the judgement given for personal development will very likely limit you to grade 2 – the requires improvement descriptor makes this clear for all key judgements: 'Other than in exceptional circumstances, it is likely that, when the school is judged as requires improvement in any of the key judgements, the school's overall effectiveness will also be requires improvement' (p. 40, S5). Similarly, if personal development is judged as grade 2, only in 'exceptional circumstances' could the school be outstanding overall (p. 40, S5).

Personal development is about the wider curriculum provided by schools, but there is a recognition by Ofsted that it is often impossible to measure the impact of personal development provision while the pupil is still at school. Thus, it is the quality of your provision that Ofsted seek to judge (paras 216–217, p. 58, S5), so focus on your provision and evidence it well.

The handbook outlines all the things you need to evidence in your SEF (para. 218, pp. 58–59, S5). Ensure you describe each point, although many of them could be combined. There is no need for a subheading for each one unless you really wish to do so. These include equality of opportunity, promoting an inclusive environment, character education and the good old British values, so loved from the previous framework. There is a lot here, so don't be afraid to really showcase what you do. A mention of the Duke of Edinburgh's Award, Cadet Forces and National Citizenship Service could be advantageous, as Ofsted actually name all three, but I'm sure you are giving your pupils all sorts of other curricular enhancements and extracurricular activities.

Preparation for the next stage of education

References to the 'next stage' education crop up several times in the inspection handbook and in several areas. It does so here. This section encompasses personal aspirations, behaviours and attitudes, together with good outcomes. You could link what you do to promote good pupil success in the next stage of their education from behaviours and attitudes to your writing about the curriculum in quality of education, to careers education and the 'Gatsby Benchmarks' under personal development. No NEETs, or NEETs below the national average, can be a persuasive factor that all these things are strong in your school, and should be mentioned wherever possible.

Spiritual, moral, social and cultural development

Although there are no judgement criteria for spiritual, moral, social and cultural (SMSC) development, and it is not judged separately, it is worth giving it its own section. In many ways, SMSC has been reduced in importance in this framework and inadequate SMSC will no longer lead to grade 4. However some parts of it, especially around radicalisation, extremism and the Prevent Agenda, are specifically mentioned in the criteria for inadequate (p. 63, S5). SMSC has now been included in 'personal development', instead of under 'overall effectiveness', as it was in the previous framework.

What is expected of you is clearly set out under separate subheadings (paras 220–223, pp. 59–61, S5), so reflect this using the subheadings for all four areas. Write this section in line with the bullet points on those pages.

As it is about provision, the 'personal development' section allows you to show off about your provision. Enjoy writing this section. I'll bet you have a lot to be proud about!

2.6. Leadership and Management

Ofsted have a new rationale for leadership and management in the EIF (para. 229, p. 64, S5). This is quite a demotion from the previous framework, about which Sir Michael Wilshaw said, 'Great leadership is at the heart of the three major reforms Ofsted is making to inspection,'[10] and put leadership and management first and foremost in inspection judgements. Just four years on, how things have changed! They will change again, but for the time being, remember the new primacy of curriculum as you write all areas of this section.

The bullets (para. 229, p. 64, S5) provide you with many of the areas you need to write about and evidence, but this section also gives prominence to other areas such as governance and safeguarding. The handbook grade descriptors for leadership and management for good (pp. 74–75, S5) are a better guide, and I would use each one as a subheading. If you do, you won't leave out subjects like governors, parents and safeguarding, and especially how leaders have conceived and implemented a curriculum bespoke to your school.

Talk up the role of the head teacher here, even though it may be the head teacher writing the SEF (I know that it's not always easy), and discuss the distributive leadership in the school.

If you are a part of a MAT, the roles and responsibilities of the school within the MAT need to be explained (paras 237–239, pp. 65–66, S5). If you are not, ignore these. This could be done at the start of the next section on governance.

There is tangential reference to partnerships in the descriptors, via a mention of trustees if you are in a MAT, but paragraphs 245 and 246 (p. 67, S5) reference partnerships more explicitly, so include it in your writing. If the use of external agencies has been used appropriately and successfully in particular areas (e.g. teaching, behaviour, SMSC), reference this in the individual section, referring to evidence of improvement. Seeking help should not be regarded as a weakness; this is about seeking particular expertise that you may not have in the school and can be presented as a positive for leadership and management.

---

10 Ofsted, *The Future of Education: Understanding the Changes* (June 2015), p. 2. Available at: https://www.gov.uk/guidance/changes-to-education-inspection-from-september-2015.

The rest of the leadership and management section is a series of sub-headings to which the handbook gives particular importance. All are included in the inadequate descriptors (p. 75, S5) and are limiting judgements for your grade. That is, fail *any* of these and you will be judged inadequate for leadership and management, and thus grade 4 overall. The following points need to be explained separately:

- Governance.

- Use of the pupil premium and its effectiveness.

- Gaming.

- Inclusion and off-rolling.

- Safeguarding.

Evidence all of them. The SEF tools in the appendices contain all the information you need. Just a few points here, mainly about safeguarding.

Be aware that leadership and management will not get its own section in your report, but the quality of leadership and management will inform other paragraphs, especially if the conclusion is requires improvement. However, the judgement given for leadership and management will very likely limit you to grade 2 – the requires improvement descriptor makes this clear for all key judgements: 'Other than in exceptional circumstances, it is likely that, when the school is judged as requires improvement in any of the key judgements, the school's overall effectiveness will also be requires improvement' (p. 40, S5). Similarly, if leadership and management is judged grade 2, only in 'exceptional circumstances' could the school be outstanding overall (p. 40, S5).

Safeguarding

Please make sure your safeguarding is top-notch. I have no sympathy with schools that make mistakes and nor will Ofsted. Keeping pupils safe is a school's first priority. To underline that expectation, safeguarding is the only part of the framework that gets a separate section in reports. Inspectors are expected to judge whether safeguarding is effective and to write a short paragraph to describe safeguarding arrangements and outcomes.

Here are some observations by school leaders who have been inspected under the EIF (all of which are thanks to the good people of #TwitterEd).

- They are much more keen on safeguarding than they were before. They will ask various people in different roles within school, regarding who is the DSL [designated safeguarding lead] and the deputy DSL. They'll check safeguarding training is up-to-date too. It's nothing bad, it's just a tad more in depth.

- I had a lot more questions about how the curriculum supports safeguarding and how we teach children to protect themselves from local priorities (child sexual exploitation and county lines), which was then followed up with staff and children.

- Not significantly different for us. Training, records and referrals were checked. Several staff were asked about dealing with concerns, whistleblowing and well-being. Children were asked how they keep safe. Inspectors asked about safeguarding through curriculum. In the phone call we were asked about local issues.

- We also got asked about the *Keeping Children Safe in Education* document.[11] One question we were asked was, 'What do you understand this section to mean?' We talked about county lines and what the main issues were for our students.

- The questions tend to get asked within deep dives (e.g. to pupils and staff). Many more people are seen now than before. Also questions were asked to lunch supervisors and other non-teaching staff. They were the usual questions about pupil-on-pupil abuse, female genital mutilation, upskirting, etc.

- I was asked to explain a case where I had made a difference, what I did and who I spoke to, all anonymised. We were also asked for a list of leavers in the last academic year and why they had left the school (checking on off-rolling, I think).

- Our safeguarding governor was interviewed in depth and they asked a whole range of staff the basic questions. They also asked pupils about online safety and healthy relationships.

- You may need to show the number of cases referred to outside agencies and the outcome – specifically, how things improved or how you further escalated it if things didn't improve.

---

11 Department for Education, *Keeping Children Safe in Education: Statutory Guidance for Schools and Colleges* (September 2019). Available at: https://www.gov.uk/government/publications/keeping-children-safe-in-education--2.

■ Ensure you have up-to-date Level 3 training certificates for DSL and deputy DSL at least. Children's views were important. Referrals and tracking were looked at, as were our recording trails. *Keeping Children Safe in Education* was asked about. Policies were asked for. Questions around safeguarding were asked to staff, parents and others in the school. It was thorough. They asked various staff, including three student teachers, what they would do if they had a concern about a child. They also asked staff about whistleblowing and well-being.

Safeguarding just has to be spot on. There really is no way round this.

Coronavirus update

The COVID-19 outbreak has seen leaders perform Herculean feats of organisation both to keep children safe and to organise their continued learning. Show that through your self-evaluation.

CHAPTER 3

AN INSPECTOR'S INSPECTION – INSPECTION METHODOLOGY

3.1. Introduction

Your lead inspector is human. Promise! The HMI and Ofsted inspectors I worked with as a team member were some of the best professionals I have ever met. They are very well trained and well acquainted with the EIF inspection methodology. Some HMI may already be veterans of many inspections in this framework, including pilot inspections, sections 8s and section 5s, while others will be fairly new to their role, although they will become more experienced as the framework develops. However, like all of us, they can be persuaded and can respond emotionally.

Some will not have led a school, but don't try to use that against them. Instead, help your inspectors to see that you realise they have lots of other experiences which equip them to perform the role effectively. There is no need to put their backs up, unless they are not inspecting by the handbook. The team inspectors may well not have subject experience. Again, accept that, but store all this information away, just in case one of your inspectors makes a mistake and you need to talk to the lead inspector or even Ofsted about their conduct.

This chapter approaches inspection from your lead inspector's point of view and discusses the methodology they will use, with a few tips on how you can use that knowledge to your advantage and uncover any unknown unknowns in the inspection process.

Before visiting your school, the person leading your inspection will receive several things from Ofsted and will be expected to look at others. Indeed, most lead inspectors will have begun their inspection preparation some weeks before, with a look over the school they have been allocated, which could easily include a perusal of your performance tables as they are public information. I remember well the wince, or appreciative nod, that this produced from me at my laptop screen. You can't help your reaction. As I say, we are all human.

Ofsted quickly abandoned their initial proposal of a half-day 'scoping visit' the day before the inspection (cue outrage from schools that inspection would be effectively two-and-half days – again, I don't think Ofsted had thought that one through). They have now settled on a 90-minute phone call instead. They state that their pilots showed that school leaders wanted this (really?). Still, you and your lead inspector are stuck with it and you both need to prepare. There are some other things your lead inspector will have to do in preparation too, and they will be under pressure on the day before they arrive. (Some will spread this prep but they only get paid for one day to prepare.)

It is important you are aware of this because you can use this information to your advantage, in your own preparation, by making things as easy as possible, while also controlling when your lead inspector receives material from you. Especially when you send them your school development plan. Make sure they receive this a couple of hours *after* you have sent them your SEF.

On a personal level, I'm poacher-turned-gamekeeper now, helping schools to keep at bay the metaphorical Ofsted foxes and hawks. I inspected many schools and led many inspections up to the end of 2017. My name is on the previous reports of those schools and I'm very proud of that work (although I admit that I was always an inspector whose glass was a fair bit more than half-full!). There is good in all schools. Therefore, I thought it would be helpful for your preparation if I detailed the methodology that your inspectors will use. It is very different to the previous framework in some ways, but similar in others.

I will organise much of this chapter with your next lead inspector very much in mind, via my own experience, but also bearing in mind the experiences of current inspectors who update me on inspection practice.

This chapter is aimed specifically at head teachers and principals, although I hope it will be interesting for others too. I will allude to HMI work and I will reference what they and Ofsted inspectors have to do, but I am not and have never been an HMI. HMI, or Ofsted inspectors who lead such inspections, would not be allowed by Ofsted to give their personal interpretations of this process in public. They would have to leave Ofsted to do so, as I did.

As an aside, being an HMI would actually have driven me spare! I observed in *Talk for Teaching* that I don't do bosses well – hence, building up and running my own company, QA South-West. Working under the crazily strict guidelines of Ofsted would never have been a bag I could have carried very far.

Good luck to HMI, though: you have my respect. HMI are almost all experienced, personable and often consummate professionals who work well with schools and inspect with great knowledge. Their previous work in supporting grade 3 and 4 schools to improve was often exemplary, and was usually much appreciated by the schools with whom they worked. Now, the appearance of regional schools commissioners has completely disrupted the process via forced academisation. In my opinion, this is the single worst thing that could happen to a school as part of the inspection process, and it is a big driver for me in writing this book. It is a pity that such excellent HMI work has almost stopped, as there is little need now. Some monitoring visits do occur, but these are almost all limited to grade 3 schools. Instead, regional schools commissioners ensure that favoured MATs will now take over the work of supporting failing schools, whether the school wants to be part of the MAT or not. The process is flawed and shot through with vested interests, powerful people and shenanigans. Having been deeply involved with schools as they tried to fight off this process (it is possible, but very, very difficult) my view here is coloured a deep shade of black.

Another digression: I hate the term 'failing schools' with a vengeance. Many of these schools are deemed to be failing by a value-added metric which means they are more likely to fail. This is desperately unfair. If a school has a greater proportion of disadvantaged pupils, because it finds itself in a more disadvantaged catchment, it is more likely to have progress scores that are below expected. It's as simple as that. All schools are inspected by a value-added measure that is applied equally to schools in very different contexts. Even under the new inspection framework, which Ofsted promised would free schools in challenging circumstances from the yoke of value-added data, early indications are that exactly the same thing is still happening. This implies that schools with more disadvantaged catchments may still be being disadvantaged by the EIF.[1] More on this later in this chapter.

To me, this is iniquitous. It is deplorable. It is unfair. It is simply not a level playing field, and it is a playing field that got much more uneven when we saw the demise of contextual value added in 2011. It is time a measure of contextual value added was brought back to give today's disadvantaged schools – and their pupils – a better chance on inspection. No pupil can feel good about being in a supposedly failing school, which is struggling because many disadvantaged pupils, just like them, are in it. There are calls from many quarters for the return of a contextual value-added measure, rather than the pure value-added measure we have now at both primary and secondary. One of those voices is the Headteachers' Roundtable (@HeadsRoundtable on Twitter), a think tank of primary and secondary head teachers who propose a 'multi year contextualised value added measure' in their *Alternative Green Paper*.[2]

OK, back to an inspector's inspection …

3.2. Pre-inspection

(This is covered in para. 65, pp. 19–20, S5.)

Before he or she arrives in your school, your lead inspector will also be expected to look at other information. They will summarise this for other inspectors via evidence forms (now electronic – Ofsted call this electronic evidence gathering, or EEG). They will examine your website, so ensure that your curriculum information is up to date and

---

1   Pippa Allen-Kinross, New inspections 'still disadvantage' less affluent schools, analysis suggests, *Schools Week* (2 November 2019). Available at: https://schoolsweek.co.uk/new-inspections-still-disadvantage-less-affluent-schools-analysis-suggests.

2   Headteachers' Roundtable, *The Alternative Green Paper: Schools That Enable All to Thrive and Flourish* (London: Schools Week, 2016), p. 12. Available at: https://headteachersroundtable.files.wordpress.com/2016/09/htrt-the-alternative-green-paper-schools-that-enable-all-to-thrive-and-flourish.pdf.

comprehensive, with the same kind of explanations about curriculum content and progress through the years that will be found in your SEF. Contextualise and explain any raw data there. Your website explanations about results should match your SEF, not your school development plan, which may contain more references to weaknesses. Add commentary to any questionnaire results that mirror the commentary in your SEF.

Inspectors will also be expected to do an Internet check to look for any other publicly available information about the school that has made the news, so do the same check yourself of the first few pages of a Google search. It will probably show nothing negative, but be forearmed if it does. Any publicly available information from other parties will also be scrutinised, such as the local authority, Department for Education or police.

In addition, they will receive your previous inspection report/monitoring letters, responses from Parent View and information about any qualifying complaints to Ofsted, which may include information about safeguarding issues and warning notices issued to the school.

That is a lot of work for your lead inspector, so if you can include a paragraph in your SEF which says, 'There is no negative information, safeguarding or otherwise, of which we are aware, on the Internet or in the local press from the local authority, Department for Education or police concerning our pupils,' it may help them to verify that their search is accurate. I always worried that I had missed something, and exactly how many pages of Google should you check as a lead inspector?

Beyond the information I have referred to above, your inspectors will have nothing else. This is what makes your self-evaluation so important because, following on from your phone call, it will be the first detailed flavour of your school that your lead inspector (by far the most important person on the team and the individual who should be the main focus of your persuasion) will see. Your phone call should anticipate your SEF and it should be able to provide handy prompts for your discussion with the lead inspector. They need to see your SEF as early as possible on the afternoon following their introductory phone call to you.

The lead inspector will also have prepared the basics of their joining instructions to their team. These will contain the intended deep dives and other trails to which they want the team to pay special attention.

Questions will have arisen from their analyses that they feel will need to be answered through the information their team collect. Your lead inspector will complete these joining instructions following their phone call to the head teacher or principal, and perhaps after they have read your SEF, if you get it to them quickly.

By 4pm, following the phone call, your lead inspector may be on their way to their hotel, if they don't travel early in the morning. The more relaxed they are feeling because their inspection preparation has gone well, the better they will be feeling about the inspection and thus, potentially, about your school. As I say, everyone in this process is human. A calm lead inspector's mind could be a favourable one, so help them! They will spend the evening and perhaps early morning (I used to) going over your SEF and the other information you will have sent and they will be in contact with their team. Throughout this time you may be in touch with your lead inspector by email and you will be sending any documents you have been asked for. This may happen on several occasions, so be prompt with replies and appear well organised, because he or she will want to be well prepared when they arrive. Keep your inspectors close but your lead inspector closer. You will hopefully reap the rewards tomorrow.

Some schools have a separate 'Ofsted portal' through which inspectors are given access to documents. Be careful here. If this contains information that shouldn't be seen pre-inspection, it could compromise some of your hard work in building your argument via your SEF. I think a password-protected Ofsted portal can be a good idea, but vet the contents of the documents that are uploaded very carefully before giving your inspectors access. It is the SEF that your lead inspector needs to see first. Explanation and contextualisation, to match the arguments in your SEF, are your watchwords.

3.3. The 90-Minute Pre-inspection Phone Call

After reading through the pre-inspection materials described in the last section, your lead inspector will be fairly nervously awaiting the call/email from the inspection support administrator at Ofsted to say that the school has been contacted. This signals that the lead inspector can go ahead with their 90-minute phone call. It is a big job in front of them and there is an enormous responsibility on their shoulders to get it right. They are the key person to persuade, and the first words you say to one another will be on the phone. Reduce their nerves while controlling your own. I know the webbed feet will be frantically paddling away on both ends of the call, but the swan must sail serenely on. It is your school, remember, not theirs. Make it obvious that they and their team will be welcome and that you are keen to show off your school.

The school will actually receive two phone calls. The first, at any time between 10.30am and 2pm, will be from the inspection support administrator at Ofsted. They will ask to speak to the head teacher/principal or the most senior member of staff. The purpose of this call is to confirm the inspection details, the number of pupils on roll, governance structures and provision other than the usual (paras 49–51, p. 15, S5).

At this stage, if you are the head teacher, arrange with Ofsted when the second phone call will take place. If you are off-site and it is possible to get back, I would do so. You can delay the call until later. Don't go cancelling out-of-school meetings on the off-chance that Ofsted will call, but do make sure that you are contactable, as always, if there is a problem. Or, even better, trust your next-in-charge to do the necessaries, but if you can get back it would be better to do the call together.

Make sure you have an Ofsted action plan and kick-start it as soon as that first call comes in. Hopefully this will include who should be there when the lead inspector calls. I would always have someone with me. They can take notes, as well as helping out, leaving you free to think. On three occasions under the old framework, when I have been supporting a school and the call has come in, I have sat passing (hopefully helpful) sticky notes to the head! Speakerphones are a boon at this time.

The second call will be from your lead inspector. This preparatory telephone conversation will be 90 minutes long and will be divided into two parts, which may actually end up as two separate calls (para. 54, p. 17, S5):

- ■ A reflective, educationally focused conversation about the school's progress since the last inspection.
- ■ A shorter inspection-planning conversation that focuses on practical and logistical issues.

Either can come first – it's up to you and your lead inspector. At this stage, show your knowledge and take control. Talk about the order of the two elements and suggest a comfort break. Your lead inspector is tasked with making relationships at this stage and will have a script to talk through. Make their job as easy as possible by recognising that they might need time to write or type. The handbook (paras 54–64, pp. 17–19, S5) gives you all the information you need about what these calls will cover and it is worth a read. Here is the experience of one head teacher which may also help:

When the office told me Ofsted were on the phone, my heart raced much as it has in any previous inspection. The mixture of nerves and excitement kick in almost instantly. This time it was heightened as I knew I wouldn't know everything expected of me, because I was substantive head and not permanent. The lead HMI had a friendly tone and it was clear from the outset that, while Ofsted clearly had their job to do, it was *our* inspection and we were in charge – i.e. if we wanted to speak as a group for clear reasons then that was fine.

The first part of the call was pretty standard and similar to previous inspections. It contained all the standard information-sharing and typical pleasantries, etc. We were told there would need to be a longer chat which we could do now or later. We asked for a call slightly later to allow us to gather information and inform staff.

During the second call, there was a rigorous exchange of information, but it wasn't an interrogation. We were very honest about where we were and had conversations, at length, about school context, the progress since the last inspection, key trails from the IDSR, school priorities, curriculum, etc. As usual, it was agreed to exchange the SEF and SIP [school improvement plan] in advance, and a list of documentation which would be required during the inspection was emailed.

As our inspection was a section 8 monitoring inspection, initially we were told they were looking for some very clear things:

- Has the school taken effective action to improve and are there clear plans in place?
- Have governors had an impact?
- Has the quality of education improved for children?
- Has the school taken appropriate steps to build an effective curriculum?

This is your first chance to sell your school and, in doing so, persuade your lead inspector of the grades and overall effectiveness you feel you deserve. Have a rigorous exchange of information and be prepared for some searching questions. Your inspection doesn't start tomorrow morning at 8am; it is already under way. Have a short prompt sheet prepared of the main things you want to get across and use your SEF information as a template for the conversation. Give your deputy/other listeners explicit permission to add information to the call; it would be good for your lead inspector to see some distributive leadership here.

Your lead inspector will have a list of possible questions to ask. Here is a flavour of the questions asked of one primary school during the first part of their phone call. This list is not exhaustive, but it is detailed, because a member of the senior leadership team (SLT) took notes (helped by the fact that the conversation was on speakerphone – highly sensible). Most of the questions are applicable to secondary schools too. There are a few notes from me *in italics*. As it was a new school, this was a section 5 inspection.

We agreed a one-hour call now and a half-hour call this afternoon – time to find things for later.

Part 1 of the phone call: school context and questions about the school's work, especially curriculum

Questions:

1. What changes are in place since the last inspection?
2. What other changes have there been to the SLT recently and what are their roles?
3. Pupil data – SEND, pupil premium, looked-after children, total on roll?
4. Prepare class lists including SEND/pupil premium.

Education focus:

5. School context – tell me about mobility/deprived/limited life experiences, engaging parental support/visits/visitors, vocabulary project, high number of SEND, attendance.

6. Tell me about progress since the last inspection.

7. How are you currently evaluating the school?

8. Strengths and weaknesses in terms of the curriculum.

Foundation subjects:

9. How do you design the curriculum? How do you ensure it covers the programmes of study?

10. Tell me about the way teaching supports pupils to learn the curriculum. How do they use assessment, and how do they remember what they are learning?

11. How do the teachers use assessment to inform planning?

12. How do you make sure the curriculum meets the needs of all children – SEND, pupil premium, behavioural needs?

Reading:

13. We'll be focusing on reading via a deep dive. *(Ofsted do in every inspection, so look at the information on what Ofsted will look for in reading (para. 87, p. 24, S5).)*

14. How do you make sure reading is a priority?

15. We have your phonics outcomes from the website – do you have the early learning goals (ELG) to hand?

16. When will phonics be taught during the visit?

17. Will there be any additional intervention in Year 1/2 for phonics?

18. We would like to hear some children read – the lowest 20%. The phonics leader needs to bring us lists of pupils who didn't meet ELG or the requirements of the phonics screening checks in Years 1 and 2. If possible, we will observe them reading with a familiar adult – we will chat with the member of staff here – the school's adult will use the right terminology. May we have two pupils from Year 1, two from Year 2 and two from Year 3? We'll need to listen to reception children in their classroom. *(There was a big focus on reading in the inspection and there will be in yours – primary or secondary.)* Could the staff member from Year 3 show them provision for phonics? We'll need to evaluate the effectiveness of support for these children.

Other questions:

19. Please would you tell me your Key Stage 2 data for last year. *(An odd request, in some ways, as the inspector would already have this. The question points to the continued, behind the scenes, focus on data. Address this in your SEF and refer to it.)*

20. Ensure quality of the curriculum – you have already told me about scrutiny and how you monitor it, so I don't need to ask.

21. Tell me about personal development for pupils – what is the offer like?

Decide on the subjects for the deep dives (one hour into the call at this point). Five subjects: reading, mathematics, science, geography and art. Are you aware of the deep dive methodology?

▨ First part is talking to you for the overview.

▨ Meet with subject leaders *(so talk to them first about what they might experience)* – where possible, before the start of school or in the afternoon before the subject is being taught.

▨ All other activities are based on the subject leaders' feedback.

▨ What is your intent?

▨ What will they be doing in Year 4/6 etc. so we can check what is actually happening in reality?

▨ Draft schedule has been made already *(the lead inspector will do this pre-inspection)* and will be finalised when you pass on timetables.

▨ Lesson visits, book scrutiny, talking to staff, talking to pupils.

Part 2 of the phone call: inspection logistics

▨ Timetables need to be uploaded to portal.

▨ We need to let parents know – Parent View (as in email).

▨ When we get the timetable – curriculum/senior leaders are welcome to take part with the inspectors in the activities/deep dives.

▨ Documentation for tomorrow – in the handbook.

▨ SEF, SDP, etc. No need to have them prior to inspection – just in the room for the day. *(I'd always counsel sending your SEF immediately – it's a tool for persuasion. Leave your SDP for them in the room, as asked.)*

▨ Policies should be on website now.

▨ Support plans need to be available for education, health and care plan (EHCP)/SEND pupils.

- Inspectors will be using laptops for data-gathering so need a power supply.
- Tea and coffee needed in base room. They will order lunch when they get here and will pay adult meal price.
- If we have any concerns during the inspection we must alert the lead inspector. They want to work with us and communicate with us, so they are asking us to show them where they will see particular activities taking place. They want to make sure we feel we have had a fair inspection.
- Agreed time of 4.30pm for another five-minute phone call after the timetables have been submitted to them.

There is lots of food for thought here!

3.4. During the Inspection

Your inspectors will arrive at 8am, and after a few introductions and pleasantries they will set to work quickly. Time is of the essence and your lead inspector will be keen to organise their team and set them off on their tasks and deep dives. However, always remember that this is *your* school and inspectors are on *your* territory, not vice versa. If there is something you wish the team to see, speak to the lead inspector and in most instances they will acquiesce.

In primary schools, inspectors may well talk to parents before and/or after school to help plan their work and confirm hypotheses. There are always fewer opportunities to speak with parents in secondary schools. Early on, inspectors will want to speak with a range of stakeholders – including senior and subject leaders, and perhaps pupils – to establish what they need to investigate during the inspection.

Inspection methodology: a flavour of the EIF from current inspectors

The notes in the section that follows are from inspectors and lead inspectors who have attended recent training. These good people can't blog or tweet about this and they need to remain anonymous – it could be a breach of their contract if they do so. Thus, I'm very grateful for the information and help they have given through some long and fascinating phone calls, emails and direct messages. Thank you to all of you – you have my sincere gratitude!

To complement their notes, a fairly short publication that will help staff to understand how Ofsted say they will inspect under this framework is *Inspecting the Curriculum*.[3] The very fact that a full document has been produced by Ofsted to explain the methodology they use in collecting evidence for quality of education only serves to underline its importance in this inspection framework. I'm sure this document will be updated as the EIF develops.

In *Inspecting the Curriculum*, Ofsted state that the inspection method reflects the connectedness of the quality of education judgement and has three overarching elements: the top-level view, deep dives and bringing it together.

The process begins with an overview (p. 4): 'inspectors and leaders start with a top-level view of the school's curriculum, exploring what is on offer, to whom and when, leaders' understanding of curriculum intent and sequencing, and why these choices were made.' *(Via the phone call, your SEF and early inspection meetings.)*

Within this, Ofsted say that inspectors will want to understand the school's context (p. 5) and the progress the school has made since the last inspection, which is important information to include in your SEF.

Then comes the deep dive (p. 4), 'which involves gathering evidence on the curriculum intent, implementation and impact over a sample of subjects, topics or aspects. This is done in collaboration with leaders, teachers and pupils. The intent of the deep dive is to seek to interrogate and establish a coherent evidence base on quality of education.'

Inspectors want to see the ambitions and intentions of senior leaders being carried out in classrooms (p. 6). They say that their mantra here is 'let's see that in action together', so be prepared to do just that in teacher and subject leader conversations.

---

3   Ofsted, *Inspecting the Curriculum: Revising Inspection Methodology to Support the Education Inspection Framework* (2019). Ref: 190024. Available at: https://www.gov.uk/government/publications/inspecting-the-curriculum.

Ofsted then go on to explain the methodology of deep dives, which includes the following elements (p. 7, original emphasis):

- evaluation of **senior leaders'** intent for the curriculum in this subject or area, and their understanding of its implementation and impact
- evaluation of **curriculum leaders'** long- and medium-term thinking and planning, including the rationale for content choices and curriculum sequencing
- visits to a deliberately and explicitly connected **sample of lessons**
- **work scrutiny** of books or other kinds of work produced by pupils who are part of classes that have also been (or will also be) observed by inspectors
- discussion with **teachers** to understand how the curriculum informs their choices about content and sequencing to support effective learning
- discussions with a group of **pupils** from the lessons observed.

Finally, in bringing it together (p. 4), 'inspectors will bring the evidence together to widen coverage and to test whether any issues identified during the deep dives are systemic. This will usually lead to school leaders bringing forward further evidence and inspectors gathering additional evidence.' *(Often on the second day.)*

At the end of day one there will be a meeting (pp. 10–11) to, among other things, allow the lead inspector to 'quality assure' the 'connectedness' of the evidence. If there is any hint of pre-judgement in the lead inspector's mind, this meeting will ensure that the evidence collected matches the grade the inspector(s) have in mind for the school. The question, 'Where do you think this school is?' is almost certain to be asked, in one form or another, in that meeting. Final judgements will be made at the end of day two, as has always been the case (p. 12).

Inspectors' notes

I will now hand over to some current inspectors to take you through the inspection process. As before, my comments appear in italics. These notes and insights will give you some forewarning and will help you not to slip up on the banana skins of the unknown unknowns.

Please note: the following can only give a foretaste of what an inspection might look like. Chapter 4 will provide more insight into practice and, together with the information in this chapter from current inspectors, raises two questions, which I wish weren't inevitable:

1. How much does value-added data and league table positions pre-determine/influence inspection results in the minds of lead inspectors?

2. How consistent are inspections and lead inspectors?

- This is a very different framework and all inspectors felt Ofsted genuinely want to shift the emphasis away from results on the two days. *(There are many possible positives; more than I first thought when the EIF was introduced. However, in one conversation with an HMI a worry of mine – that published results will still play a significant part – surfaced in a comment that 'we can't ignore published results'. These results, of course, are dependent on value-added data and take no account of context – which is why a factual but compelling context statement in your SEF is so important.)*

- Inspectors must not comment on progress. If they talk about progress data on inspection, apparently 'a big red buzzer goes off at Ofsted HQ'! *(A quote from a senior HMI speaking at a training event! This remains an enormous concern for me, especially for schools in challenging circumstances. If progress data cannot be discussed, all that is left is attainment data, which would tip the scales significantly towards advantage. My counsel is to be wary of inspection leaders with fixed mindsets and prepare persuasive explanations and arguments in a very positive SEF.)*

- Inspectors must not ask to see internal data but must look at it if it is presented. *(If someone is refusing to look at what you wish them to see, call the Ofsted helpline and complain during your inspection.)*

- One lead inspector commented how difficult she and others around her table thought it would now be to get outstanding, as it is not a best fit any more. Every single area of good has to be achieved, and a lot more.

- There was a focus on zero tolerance in training. If inspectors perceive that zero tolerance is being backed by increased exclusions, and especially any hint of off-rolling, woe betide the school. *(If so, that would be great news.)*

- High workload expectations will be frowned upon. If you are still doing more than six data drops per year, you had better be prepared to explain why.

▨ A typical first day might include:

1. Briefly meet with SLT for introductions and with middle leaders to get a sense of intent.

2. Deep dives take place with middle leaders, not generally with senior staff. *(You can have input here. Take control: if you want a senior leader in a deep dive, stand your ground. Inspectors can't insist on only subject leaders in deep dives, although it might give the impression that your subject leaders don't know their stuff. It's up to you. A difficult decision, I know, but exercise that control if you need to.)*

3. Meet with pupils early, maybe even before deep dives.

4. Meet with the same middle leaders at lunchtime to discuss the morning's work.

5. Less of an emphasis on senior leaders early on. The inspection is front-loaded with collecting information that can be 'connected' in the team's discussions.

▨ Intent is now very important. It is key for middle leaders (especially subject leaders) to understand this and key for them to be able to articulate to an inspector what intent means in their area and for the school as a whole. How consistent is the vision? Inspectors will check that this is monitored and quality assured as a part of your curriculum monitoring. In terms of that monitoring, quality assurance of the curriculum appears to be a frontrunner for the new monitoring of progress. On the first day, subject leaders need to talk the talk, especially around curriculum intent. *(If your subject leaders can't articulate intent well, it will be hard to get good overall in your inspection.)*

▨ Sequencing in the curriculum is also very important. It is therefore essential to evidence how the curriculum builds knowledge and skills over time. How much do pupils know now compared to what they did, and why? How does the curriculum contribute to that as a pupil passes through the school? These questions will be asked to many people, including to the pupils. *(Do you need to perform a curriculum review, audit and then continue to review it via quality assurance throughout the year? (Up to you, but there are workload issues.)*

▨ In the first year, if a school says it has not yet had time to fully implement its curriculum plans, the lead inspector must call the Ofsted duty desk to discuss transitional arrangements.

▨ Deep dives are effectively going to be the new lesson observations, which are now called 'lesson visits' and not 'observations'. *(I think someone at Ofsted must have been reading* Talk for Teaching!*)* There will be no random or whole-school lesson visit focus any more. Lesson visits will be with subject leaders, in the main, and will only be targeted at the subjects chosen for a deep dive, unless a different issue arises.

- However, in primary, reading will always be a deep dive, plus mathematics and probably one other foundation subject. In secondary, it will typically be four to six subjects, including maths and English. During these deep dives, inspectors will select six books per subject and ask questions of subject leaders such as, 'Why are you doing this work now?' and 'How does this build on what has come before, and how does it lay the foundations for what will come?' They will ask similar questions of pupils and look to see curriculum progression in books.

- The new buzzword is 'connectedness'. It has replaced 'triangulation' but is essentially the same thing.

- No subject will be reported on individually; all deep dives will go towards assessing whole-school quality of education. In these deep dives, the national curriculum is very much part of the toolkit. Inspectors will be expected to ask subject-specific questions around the national curriculum. *(Therefore, you are quite likely to get an inspector who is not a specialist in your subject and may well never have taught it. Good luck to inspectors in knowing all the national curriculum, GCSE and A level specs well enough to do this! It could give subject leads an advantage.)*

- There will be a focus in deep dives on how schools organise learning to help SEND and disadvantaged pupils. *(Is this back to a re-focus on differentiation? Where does whole-class teaching fit in here? Explain your teaching model clearly; you do not have to get your teachers to change their teaching for the inspection.)*

- Following a deep dive, there may well be discussions with teachers in each deep dive subject around how the learning has been sequenced. There may also be discussions with pupils, drawn from the lessons visited, focusing on what they have learned and how much more they know now compared to before the lesson. They will be expected to bring their books with them.

- Many speakers in our training said, 'Let's wait to see how this framework pans out.' *(Ofsted will be feeling their way into this framework for quite a long time.)*

- Reading is now of even higher importance than before. It will form a deep dive at primary, but it will also inform deep dive questions at secondary. Expect questions like, 'What are you doing in your subject to promote reading?' and 'How is the school promoting reading across the curriculum?'

OK, I couldn't ask about everything, but I hope this gives you a sense of what the new inspection framework will look like to an inspector. Let's see if the reality matches the training, and if this framework, the HMI and lead inspectors really are more glass half-full, especially towards schools in challenging circumstances. Good luck, folks!

Early indications are that inspectors are *not* being glass half-full to schools in challenging circumstances. A *Schools Week* analysis of inspection reports makes pretty sobering reading, with a similar pattern of grades to the previous framework coming through: more schools in challenging circumstances in requires improvement and more advantaged schools being classed as good.[4] This was from a small sample, so I hope this trend does not continue.

Final feedback

All being well, your lead inspector will have ensured that nothing in the final feedback meeting comes as a surprise, as they should have followed the expectations contained in the Ofsted handbook and kept you, as head teacher, fully up to date. Despite any bad news, hopefully the parting will be on amicable terms – it is possible. In my inspection career, I'm pleased to say that I never had a complaint from a school. However, I have been involved as a team member when a complaint has been made, and the pressure on the lead inspector can be horrendous if these are personal. Avoiding complaints is down to the way lead inspectors inspect, and I'm gratified to see some evidence that complaints may be reducing following the contracting of inspectors directly to Ofsted.

Following the final team meeting, feedback will be given to the school in accordance with the handbook (para. 118, p. 30, S5). A range of people can attend the meeting, depending on the type of school (maintained, academy, MAT, etc.). All grades are provisional and there are caveats about with whom the report should be shared. Note the word 'should': there is no 'must' in the handbook for not sharing further than Ofsted's suggestions. I'm not sure what would happen to a school if they shared the report more widely, but it is probably sensible not to test this too far. Grades can change between inspection and publication, but that is not

---

4   Allen-Kinross, New inspections 'still disadvantage' less affluent schools.

very common. Just make sure that any shares are marked with 'restricted and confidential', as suggested in the handbook (para. 119, p. 31, S5).

The handbook also contains information as to procedures and monitoring of requires improvement, inadequate (and therefore a category for concern, as are all grade 4 schools), special measures and serious weaknesses schools (paras 121–143, pp. 31–36, S5).

3.5. After the Inspection

After the submission of the report by the lead inspector, quality assurance takes place next. Ofsted state that, 'Typically, schools will receive an electronic version of the final report within 25 working days of the end of the inspection. In most circumstances, the final report will be published on Ofsted's website within 30 working days' (para. 148, p. 36, S5). In practice, and unless the school is placed in a category of concern, when a longer period is usually required for school comments, this timescale is often shorter.

The complaints procedure is set out in the handbook (paras 155–156, p. 37, S5). Again, I will wish you good luck with any complaints. Having been involved with many, Ofsted's procedures are stacked against complaining schools and there is no formal appeals procedure. Ofsted quality assure complaints against Ofsted. But five years of Ofsted being completely right about the grading of every single inspection they have carried out is simply not possible and points to terrific hubris on the part of the inspectorate. This is something that really needs to change and an independent adjudicator is desperately needed.

Raise any problems you encounter during the inspection with your lead inspector first of all. Inspection problems, especially those concerning the behaviour of other inspectors on the team, can usually be resolved without too much friction. However, if this conversation doesn't go to your satisfaction, or the problem is actually with the lead inspector and you can't get them to listen, my advice is to contact the Ofsted helpline as soon as you are sure that the team is not inspecting according to the handbook – that is, during the inspection on the first day, if you can. Call the lead inspector into your office and explain that you are going to do this and outline the reasons why. You have every right to do this. Talk to the HMI on duty desk; they may transfer you to a more senior colleague if they feel it is necessary. Leaving worries until after the inspection is to be faced with Ofsted's complaints procedure, and that is not a comfortable position for a school to find itself in. You will not change your grade.

CHAPTER 4

A SCHOOL'S INSPECTION

4.1. First-Hand Experiences of Inspection: The Good, the Bad and the Downright Ugly

All the experiences in this chapter are from a range of people in schools that have been inspected. So far, I have peppered this book with schools' experiences of EIF 2019, but I will exemplify further here. Throughout the writing of *Taking Control 2*, I have been fortunate, through Twitter, to have had the help of many individuals who have recounted their experiences – I'm grateful to them all. They have to remain anonymous, but this section is entirely down to these completely wonderful people. As before, my notes appear in italics.

1. A head teacher's experience in a large primary school

(Two days. 470 pupils on roll.)

Section 5 inspection. One HMI and two Ofsted inspectors, plus one additional (senior) HMI on day one undertaking a quality assurance role. *(Don't be thrown if you get extra bodies – it often happens. Not to worry you too much, but HMCI and the secretary of state for education have even been known to turn up!)*

The phone call

Two parts as per the handbook (para. 54, p. 17, S5):

- A reflective, educationally focused conversation about the school's progress since the last inspection.

- A shorter inspection-planning conversation that focuses on practical and logistical issues.

The lead inspector and I agreed that this would be carried out as two separate conversations with a break in-between. The handbook states, 'In total, these conversations are likely to last around 90 minutes' (para. 55, p. 17, S5). In our case, this was over two hours but at my request (or insistence!) – ensuring an understanding of the unique context of this academy was absolutely crucial. The lead inspector was in total agreement and gladly allowed more time.

Part 1: A reflective, educationally focused conversation about the school's progress since the last inspection

In addition to context (EAL speakers, deprivation, crime, mobility, etc.), we discussed:

- The journey from the previous inspection.

- The progress made overall and the key/main steps taken to ensure rapid and sustained improvement.

- Our current strengths and priorities, including self-evaluation judgements.

- Our curriculum intent and the rationale underpinning it ('Our pupils need ...').

- Our curriculum implementation and the rationale underpinning it – for example, sequencing, consistent pedagogical strategies used across the academy ('Our pupils need ...').

Part 2: A shorter inspection-planning conversation that focuses on practical and logistical issues

The first part of this call was much more procedural and followed the structure in the handbook (paras 59–64, pp. 18–19, S5).

Prior to the second call, as requested, I sent the lead inspector the time-table for each class with the subject being taught in each slot clearly labelled (e.g. 'history' rather than the topic). We then used this to choose the deep dive subjects together (in addition to reading and maths) based on what subjects were being taught during the inspection – we went with history and PE. We then worked through the logistical implications of this. I made absolutely certain that while teachers were out of class involved in deep dives, the other Ofsted inspectors would not be observing in their classrooms as the lessons would be covered by teaching assistants/others as a result of the inspection and would not therefore demonstrate typicality. Again, the lead inspector was very appreciative of this and ensured that the inspection timetable would reflect this. I felt this was an affirmation of the rapport and shared understanding built in part 1 of the phone call.

After the second call, I sent the lead inspector our school improvement plan along with a further three key documents that I had asked if she would kindly read and share with the team prior to inspection. Again, she was more than happy to do so. This was vital to the inspectors' understanding of the academy's context. The documents were the curriculum overview, language development overview and reading overview.

Overviews they really are! A maximum of three pages each and mostly bullet points, charts and so on. At this point I felt pleased that the lead inspector had invested so much time in discussing the above with me. I was about to feel very redundant for the next two days! (*I have heard similar comments from many head teachers. It is not about SLT any more; the expectations have been transferred to subject leaders.*)

Deep dives

Deep dives were sequenced like this:

- Meeting with the subject leader:
    - Curriculum intent – rationale behind approach(es).
    - Sequencing – when and how?
    - Impact – assessment and next steps.
- Lesson visits with subject leader:
    - Testing everything shared during the meeting.
    - Lots of discussion about what was seen to validate leaders' knowledge, evaluative judgements and consistency.
- Meeting with teachers who were seen during lesson visits without the subject leader. As with the subject leader, the inspector tested teachers' knowledge of:
    - Curriculum intent – rationale behind approach(es).
    - Sequencing – when and how?
    - Impact – assessment and next steps.
- Key questions:
    - Pedagogy – what? Why? CPD?
    - What was taught before? What will come next? Why?

Discussions and questions posed during those discussions

Intent and implementation

Curriculum design, coverage and appropriateness:

- How is the curriculum intent decided and communicated?
- How does the curriculum intent reflect the context and the most common barriers to learning?

- How articulate are teachers and support staff in *why* and *how* in addition to *what* is taught?

- How is assessment used to inform curriculum design and sequences of learning?

Curriculum delivery:

- How consistently does teaching reflect the curriculum intent?

- How do lessons develop pupils' communication, social and oracy skills alongside the content being taught?

- For each subject – what is taught? When? How? Why?

Impact:

- Attainment and progress (including national tests, assessments, IDSR). (*This can't be ignored, hence my advice around explaining the data in your SEF.*)

- Reading, reading, reading!

- How is early reading prioritised? How effective is the approach?

- How do we engage pupils and develop a love of reading?

- Are pupils' books pitched appropriately and changed regularly? Links to phonic knowledge.

- Are there high expectations of the level of texts pupils read at home? How engaged/aware are parents?

- For pupils who don't/can't read at home, how do we ensure access to reading to an adult regularly and reading for pleasure?

- What about pupils who fall behind?
  - Interventions? How are they designed?
  - How do we know they are effective?
  - How is the curriculum adapted for these pupils?
  - How is the curriculum adapted to prevent an increase in the number of these pupils?

Teaching (pedagogy) – contribution to delivering the curriculum as intended:

- How effective is training for *all* teaching *and* support staff – for example, in the effective use of strategies relating to curriculum intent, in the delivery of phonics and in response to the most common SEND needs?

- How are teachers' skills in subject-specific delivery audited, developed and shared?

Assessment (formative and summative):

- How is assessment used to inform curriculum design and sequences of learning?

- For each subject – how are end of key stage expectations broken down into each year group?

- For each subject – how do specific skills look different in each year group – for example, the use of pencil, ink, charcoal and pen in art and design, or the use of knowledge about an artefact in history?

- How do teachers adapt the curriculum in response to the needs of individual SEND pupils (e.g. EHCPs, SEND targets)? How are these needs communicated and evaluated?

- How is formative assessment used to ensure timely support/intervention/challenge?

Personal development:

- In what depth is personal development coherently planned and sequenced?

- How aligned is the approach and delivery to the overall curriculum intent?

- How consistent and embedded is the provision? What is the impact on pupils?

- How are links made within and between subjects to enhance pupils' SMSC development?

- Do pupils benefit from first-hand, memorable experiences as a basis for learning in context?

- How are pupils' talents and interests identified and developed?

- How does the provision reflect the school/community context?

Behaviour and attitudes:

- How do we ensure that pupil/academy-specific behaviour management strategies are clearly communicated and consistently implemented?

- How effective is training for all teaching and support staff?

- Can pupils articulate how positive behaviour and attitudes are developed/encouraged/rewarded?

- How are we encouraging attendance and punctuality? What is the impact?

- Can we demonstrate that fixed-term exclusions are a last resort?

- How do we develop pupils' resilience, independence, communication and risk-awareness/risk-taking, including when tasks are demanding and particularly for the highest attaining pupils?

Leadership and management:

- Are leaders' ambitions/expectations of what all pupils can achieve (including SEND, looked-after children and vulnerable groups) consistently high?

- Is there a tangible, consistent culture of safeguarding?

- Are all staff aware of local and/or academy-specific vulnerabilities/safeguarding issues?

- How do leaders check that all staff understand and act swiftly in response to all concerns and signs of vulnerability/risk as a result?

- How do leaders ensure that newly appointed staff have the knowledge and understanding to keep children safe, particularly if their training was completed elsewhere?

- How are newly qualified teachers and other members of staff supported, particularly in relation to academy-specific pedagogy, approaches and policies?

- Can all subject leaders – for every subject – articulate the intent and implementation section? (*It really must be for every subject – foundation as well as core subjects.*)

- How do leaders decide on policy/procedure content (e.g. curriculum, marking, planning)?

- What measures are taken to ensure staff are well supported? How do we ensure that meaningful engagement takes place with staff at all levels, including regarding workload?

- Do those responsible for governance understand their statutory duties?

- Are those responsible for governance able to link questions/challenges and visits to key improvement priorities?

- Do those responsible for governance hold leaders to account by following up responses to questions/challenges, including by looking at evidence first hand?

Keeping on track: meetings with the lead inspector

Meetings with the lead inspector were clearly timetabled pre-inspection, but may not have happened if we hadn't actively sought them during the inspection. No criticism of the team at all and no reflection on the conduct of the inspection – purely time (i.e. a lack of)! Be a nuisance – you need to know their thoughts and trails as often and in as much detail as possible. (*Such an important point here – take control!*)

End of day one meeting: around 90 minutes observing the inspection team's meeting regarding findings and trails. No judgement terminology used but evidence made their interim judgements clear. Make notes, brief staff and ensure any additional evidence relating to the content of day two is ready for the following morning.

Final feedback: exactly as detailed in the handbook (paras 118–120, pp. 30–31, S5). I requested that all SLT were present (for their development) and so that we could take copious notes!

Addendum (*and very interesting for schools in challenging circumstances*): we pushed for some grade 1s – and got it in one area! Our inspection team were spot on regarding data. Attainment – particularly at Key Stage 1 – is significantly below the national average, but we had nailed that and explained it in the phone call. Attainment is very low (from very low beginnings on entry to the school) but progress is very strong. They understood the context and agreed. (*Big sigh of relief here, but the school's knowledge and preparation had been very good.*)

2. A head teacher's experience in a three-form entry junior school

(Three Ofsted inspectors on day one and two on day two.)

Very knowledgeable lead inspector and most of my work was on the initial phone call and 'keep in touch' sessions. Very short subject leader meetings followed by plenty of time in classrooms, talking to teachers and children while looking through books. The only data conversation was the initial call summarising Key Stage 2 outcomes.

The only issue was timetabling the deep dives: six deep dives on day one meant four middle leaders (and strong teachers) out of class for almost the whole morning. I complained and it was reduced to five. This did mean that some teachers had lots of lesson visits though! (*If this is the lead inspector's thinking, be aware of possible problems and raise them in the pre-inspection planning phone call.*)

Class teachers did nothing to prepare. Middle leaders needed training in talking about curriculum design and articulating strategy.

(*There is such helpful detail in this experience. I'm very grateful to my writer for recording what happened!*)

3. An experienced primary teacher's point of view

Our inspection was not what anyone was expecting. I think many people thought the days of inspectors ignoring teachers when they say hello in the corridor and ignoring teachers in front of pupils if they politely ask, 'Would you like to see my tracking, scheme of work and so on?' had gone. They haven't.

The team brutally interrogated whole departments for 45 minutes about the curriculum and then, right at the end, threw in a very misleading question about safeguarding. Five teachers all said the same thing afterwards: 'She confused us all and then, before we could answer properly, she said, "Shall I put you out of your misery?"'

They want to know what all the middle leaders are doing, how and why. They want to know what the teachers are doing, how and why. Then that the middle leaders know everything about the teachers. Then they check all of the above with pupils to see if it joins up. (*Connectedness.*) They also test how the curriculum progresses from each key stage, even that secondary staff know exactly what has gone on at Key Stage 2 in their subject area. All I can say is what a lot of people have said: it was very intense and nothing like what they had anticipated. Don't trust them! I feel they used a lot of sneaky, underhand tactics on staff.

Also (although I didn't fall for this, I'm sure a lot of staff did), on the morning of the first day they came to the staff briefing and were all smiles and laughter. The lead inspector insisted that if there were any problems, they wanted to know about it – kind of setting the scene that it would be a positive experience. The mood seemed good. Well, it had all changed by breaktime …

(A decidedly unhappy and difficult experience. It highlights the differences in approach of inspection teams – you have to be prepared for something like this, even though it isn't typical. If you must fight dirty as a leader, then fight dirty. Talk first with your lead inspector if something like this is happening, but if you don't get the joy you are seeking, call the Ofsted helpline. Explain you are having problems with your inspection team and ask to speak to an HMI. Don't be fobbed off and ask to speak to someone as senior as possible. Complaints afterwards will not change your grade. I'm especially grateful to my writer here – this can't have been easy.)

4. The experience of a primary subject leader – deep dives and all

(Three inspectors on the first day and two on the second. Two-form entry primary school.)

I'm a subject lead in foundation subjects. They did deep dives into history, science, reading and maths, and a shallow dive into PE and phonics. (*A 'shallow dive' is definitely a thing, although nowhere are they mentioned in the handbooks. I'm assuming it is a less detailed look at a couple of foundation subjects.*)

While I feel that the overall judgement is probably fair given where we are on our journey with our wider curriculum, the deep dive aspects were horrendous for subject leads. The questioning was really intense: it was very apparent that we were only to answer the questions directly. They were totally uninterested in hearing us talk around our subjects, cutting us off a couple of times. We all felt totally inadequate for not having spent much time (four weeks in) doing learning walks and book scrutinies for our subjects (history and science). We also found them typing on laptops to be really distracting.

They observed lessons for no more than a couple of minutes at a time. The inspector asked to read with a lower-ability child who probably wouldn't achieve the phonics screening check. He said that the child had really struggled and couldn't blend even CVC [consonant vowel consonant] words. He said he wanted to see her receive an intervention the next day, which was fine, but he didn't turn up to watch the intervention despite it being on his timetable. Had he turned up, he would have seen the child segmenting and blending beautifully. Perhaps inspectors need to understand that taking a 5-year-old girl who has never met them before to a small room, expecting her to read (while looking very serious in a suit) is not conducive to a good reading session. (*Be aware of these situations and what you can do, especially subject leads who may be alone with an inspector. Challenge the methodology. If you are still unhappy, have the courage to stop the deep dive and say you need to speak to your head teacher. Take control if you find yourself in a situation in which you feel uncomfortable on behalf of the children or the staff.*)

Overall, subject leaders who were chosen for a deep dive were made to feel really terrible about their areas of the curriculum. I hope Ofsted realise that we are not paid for this – we have multiple subjects to lead and we don't receive any extra planning time or extra money.

(Awkward and difficult. Again, I'm grateful to my writer for revealing this. Subject leads can be faced with uncomfortable situations, yet they are trusting the inspector to inspect properly. A subject leader in this position may not be aware of what they can do. This is a power imbalance between a subject leader and an experienced Ofsted inspector, and that is a hard position for a middle leader to find themselves in. So, leaders, if your subject leads are experiencing practice on a deep dive which they disagree with, give them the permission to take control and seek help from you.)

5. A primary school head teacher's experience of inspection

(Two inspectors for two days. Over 200 pupils on roll.)

Day one

Deep dive in phonics/early reading/maths/history on day one but then asked for discussions from geography and art/design and technology leads to support our topic-based learning on day two.

It was very intense. The inspectors were probing and asked why we taught what we did and how, how we supported new staff, how leaders supported staff and how leaders knew what was going on where. They also dropped safeguarding, well-being and whistleblowing questions into discussions.

They talked to lots of children and looked at books too. Luckily, we had kept books from the previous year as four weeks into a new term there is little work in current books. They were not interested in marking at all. *(It is well worthwhile keeping at least some books from the previous year.)*

Because the inspection was run so efficiently, with a very detailed time-table, we could effectively see where they were going and what they were looking at throughout the day.

Day two

The inspectors dipped into foundation subjects much more and wanted to see evidence of reading being used to support SEND children in lessons. In some lessons they were in and out within five to ten minutes once they had seen what they needed to see.

Both inspectors were very 'human' and understood the day-to-day running and constraints/problems of a primary school. Both had previously been head teachers. We got a sense that to a point they were finding their feet with the new framework. It was stressful but luckily we had all of the basics there. We all went home very happy.

(A good experience and a good understanding team. Thank you to my writer for showing what an inspection should be like for all. Tough but fair. And to be fair to Ofsted, most inspections are very much like this.)

6. A geography subject leader's experience of a deep dive in a small secondary school

(Three inspectors for two days.)

Several meetings with the SLT on general running, policies, etc. – they wanted evidence of everything.

Those departments involved in deep dives had head of department interviews focused on curriculum pathways and how they impact on planning and structure in the future and how we, as teachers, meet our pupil premium needs. Each deep dive was a maximum of 20 minutes of observation within the department. The inspectors made notes, spoke to students and looked at work. We all produced context documents, alongside slides of lessons and seating plans. They selected four students, mainly pupil premium, to be invited for a group chat with the inspectors. Books were taken for work scrutiny which was carried out with the head of department.

Teachers involved in deep dives were also interviewed for about half an hour in a group setting. You had to be very confident with where your curriculum was going and how it overlapped from Key Stage 3 to Key Stage 5. (*Subject leaders in secondary schools need to be up to date with how Key Stage 3–4 learning impacts on Key Stage 5, and how Key Stage 5 builds on prior learning in both key stages.*)

For us, it was generally a good experience, but as we all know, if you have consistency and know the kids and the curriculum, you will be OK.

7. A head teacher's experience of a primary grade 4 inspection

(Two inspectors for two days. Over 200 pupils on roll.)

The process was very busy but didn't involve me as head that much during the day. They wanted to do lesson observations with subject leaders, but as my English lead also leads history we had to cover her class for most of the day on the first day to release her. She is my strongest teacher so they didn't see our best classroom practice, which was annoying. The same for our maths lead – again, one of my strong teachers.

We were due an inspection from December last year, so our focus had to be on the old framework. A lovely recently qualified teacher (RQT) with a fine art degree, who leads art, had to partake in one of our deep dives. She has only been observed as part of her development, not as a leader, so if it hadn't been such high stakes her meeting with Ofsted would have been great development. However, in reading our report, it was the lack of strength in subject leaders which pulled us down. Everyone else was mentioned as a strength, but leadership in art was mentioned as a weakness.

I now have to manage this with her so she isn't too demoralised, while also strengthening her leadership before Ofsted come back. I don't necessarily disagree with their judgement. We were an inadequate school and have had lots of instability. We've made improvements and we're on the right track, but you can't turn around teaching, rewrite a whole curriculum (there was nothing) and get everyone up to scratch on everything in less than two years. The report recognised lots of strengths, and I know we have lots to do. My only concern is that in a one-form entry school, people are recognisable, so the impact is on individual teachers, when in fact it's me, and all of us as a whole, who should have to shoulder that responsibility. An RQT with no teaching and learning responsibility or release time can't be held responsible across the school.

(A decent inspection overall, but that focus on subject leaders in smaller schools worries me – and I know it keeps some head teachers and subject leaders awake at nights. I don't think Ofsted have thought through these possible consequences sufficiently, and I'm thankful to my writer for bringing this out. If this issue might affect you, address it as best you can in the pre-inspection phone call.)

And finally, a very detailed, blow-by-blow account of an inspection in a primary school. There is lots of useful information and tips here.

8. The experience of a primary head teacher

(HMI/lead inspector and two Ofsted inspectors for two days. Larger than average, two-form entry primary school in an urban area of deprivation.)

The pre-inspection phone calls

10.30am: First came the admin call – they asked for names of pertinent leaders, asked questions around additional provision, wraparound provision, numbers on roll and other basic information. I was told that the lead inspector would ring soon. In addition the email address was confirmed for portal login details, parent letters and so on, to come direct to head teacher.

Note: Have a crib sheet containing all the key information the section 5 handbook says you need. Know what it says so you have easy and immediate answers.

11am: HMI/lead rings – they know your school from external data sources and the website. I suggest that the website is a key tool in the battle. Personal observation: my name is easily googled and comes up as the first hit – I think they had done that too! This is the time to start building rapport. The conversation is spread across 90 minutes and in two parts. The first call was logistics, plus governance, classes, school times, timetable, leaders' names and subjects. We were already beginning to consider the curriculum through how the day is spread out. We agreed on a longer curriculum philosophy and 3I's [intent, implementation, impact] call at 2.15pm.

Note: Have your class timetables in a zip folder ready to send immediately. The HMI/lead has to produce a timetable for the two days, so the quicker they get this, the more organised the school looks, and the easier it is for the HMI/lead to construct their timetable. We also mutually agreed that I would send the SEF, SIP and deeper analysis of some unvalidated data they had. Two points here: only send what they ask for and send it straight away. 'Live' or 'working' documents are believable, and later helped to convince them that we know our school, monitor effectively and our action plans are tight and precise – that all-important capacity to improve. (*Super advice – really excellent!*)

HMI shared email address – I never actually put anything on the portal in the end. We swapped a couple of clarification emails about timetables before the 2.15pm call. Draft timetable was emailed to me before that second phone call.

Note: Deep dives need to include lesson visits. If you have a stronger area of the curriculum that isn't English or maths, make sure it is happening on the days you are likely to be inspected. The very organised head teachers could even jiggle the timetable so they had a geography lesson good to go when the call comes. We didn't, so deep dives were planned in RE and PE on top of reading, writing and maths. These were no-brainers given that everyone gets early reading and our average outcomes fall well below national averages in other areas.

2.15pm: Second call. We discussed the draft timetable – the lead inspector used the staff list I'd already sent to populate the deep dive schedule. I also used this call as an opportunity to paint the school's context – the stuff you wouldn't see on websites and social media: seven heads in six years, significant staff turnover, school passed from pillar to post, I am the stability, etc. Other heads may have less to say but never assume they know – HMI and leads are busy people, not oracles.

Note: Staff on deep dives will ideally need all morning or all afternoon out. We were fortunate to have the capacity to do this, but I'm not sure how smaller schools or leaders with many hats would do it. Also, there is no lesson visit to the leader who is being covered – but their books and children had better tell a good story if needed!

Curriculum discussion – if you have curriculum content on your website then you had better know it, and know it in a way such that you don't have to read it verbatim. I have heard that other schools have passed the phone between leaders, but I took the entire call regarding the intent, implementation and impact of our curriculum. I painted an honest picture of a work in progress that was tested repeatedly across the two days.

Note: Head teacher means head *teacher* during the phone call – or it did in our context and call. However, if I weren't currently a subject lead in our school, I would have had very little to do with the inspection team on day one of our inspection.

By 3.15pm, the phone calls were done, the timetable agreed and the arrival time arranged. Time to brief staff.

Note: Share the timetable and, if you're due an inspection, drip-feed key elements of the EIF into briefings and CPD. When they see themselves on the timetable, staff should know implicitly what is being looked at, why and how. Make sure there is a key message of typicality: don't do anything different – it won't work! (*Again, excellent advice: trying to put on a show really won't work.*)

However, in our context some staff still go 'on show' when somebody comes into the room and they feel they need to 'perform' for the audience. It isn't even a conscious reaction – it's a habit they have got into. Two examples of this would be: teaching assistants talking when the teacher is talking so they look as if they are having an active impact on pupils' listening and understanding; and teachers talking for too long when pupils clearly understand and look keen to get stuck in. This impacts on progress and challenge. Get your culture right – but you won't be able to do that the night before inspection!

Day one

Logistics notes and advice

Save car park spaces, get them a big room – have tea, coffee and restrooms close at hand. A map of the school (depending on size) will be asked for – help them to orientate in larger schools. Attention to detail – where are the swipe doors? Do you have spare fobs if needed? (*A small but important point: I have found myself struggling to get into areas of a school because I haven't had the correct key fob.*)

Everything they do now is electronic, so Wi-Fi codes, plugs, sockets and so on are all very important. We had a spare room but it wasn't the most inviting. If I did it all again (when!) and had more time to plan, I would showcase all the work and key messages I wanted them to see so it was in their faces every time they went back to the room. (*I have seen schools do this very effectively on inspections I have led.*)

If you ensure the inspection runs smoothly, and if you can make their job easier through forethought and planning, then your school looks organised and efficient. It's not just about cakes and doughnuts – it's about efficiency.

The welcome and arrival is still important – it sets the tone. Ask office staff to check badges, sign people in, hand over fire and safeguarding documents that need to be read and so on. (*But make it seem natural – no big shows. This is business as usual.*)

Two minutes small talk, then discuss the logistics. Essentially, the team want to get into the room, get onto the Wi-Fi and introduce themselves to one another. They have got about 20 minutes to do this and don't want to waste it with you! Know this – they will appreciate it. (*I loved it when a school was sensitive to this. As a lead inspector you are unlikely to have met your team before. The team are under pressure. However, if there is something you need to say as a school, be brief and state it during the small talk.)*

8.20am: The usual introductions to staff. This was the nice bit – the HMI/lead showed that they had a picture of the school from our conversations and the team were genuinely there to help improve things for our pupils. The staff felt reassured (I think) and as the inspection continued they did so with the same level of integrity, professionalism and a little empathy when needed – or as much as the EIF and code of conduct would allow for. I would say that our team were professional but human. The HMI/lead and two other inspectors were either in the job or not too far removed from the reality of the job and our contexts. I'm not sure whether this was by design or luck.

8.30am: Hold on to your hats, because it's now *full on*!

The HMI/lead clarified a few curriculum points and explored our working relationships and roles as an SLT a little further.

An inspector checked the single central record (SCR) and asked a lot of questions to check the record-keeper's knowledge. They asked about checks from SLT, timeliness, supporting policies, overseas checks, right to work and so on. They then selected two random staff members and wanted to see files/documents to cross-reference with SCR information. It all linked up – a big tick for safeguarding!

Note: It is still essential that the SCR is right, but they will also look in depth at how the systems behind it function. You can't just think about pulling it together when you believe you might be due – it must be a working document and a lived practice.

An inspector checked the breakfast club (safeguarding, organisation, ratios, etc.), then the pupils arrived and they began to chat to parents.

Note: You must still send parent letters, and Parent View is there to gather parents' views. Only three out of over 300 families responded for us, so the playground chats with inspectors became important. On the second day we *may* have been at the main gate directing some key parents towards the inspectors! (*I'm smiling. I know this happened on some of my inspections, and I sometimes laughed later with the head teacher about it!*)

Deep dives

Meeting with the subject leader: 30 minutes. Make sure they know their stuff! ▪ Subject knowledge. ▪ Content knowledge. ▪ Pedagogical knowledge. Tough in smaller schools, perhaps?	Does the intent of the curriculum area match the overall school vision? Where does it come from (probably development matters and national curriculum at primary) and how is it broken down? They asked to see long- and medium-term plans (if there were any) and any progression documents – they wanted to know how what is set out on paper translates into what the children are doing daily. What happens if we need to deviate from plans? Essentially, how do you ensure 'keep up not catch up' or prevent widening gaps? Your models for delivery and pedagogical practice are as important as the pieces of paper – very big on how it all fits together and works (or will work) in harmony. If the subject is still developing, then the inspector's perceived ability of the subject leader to improve things is crucial. (*Pressure here.*)
Lesson visits (minimum of three) across a range of year groups and key stages, including early years (with subject leader): approximately one to two hours.	We'll come in, we'll come out and then we'll come back in again! It's a lesson visit, not a teacher observation (there may be some staff who still don't get that). They want to see learning. Typicality is tested. Learning behaviours for behaviour and attitudes are scrutinised. Pitch and pace of the lesson is always important.

Embedded processes and resources. Maximum learning.	Is the lesson in that 'Goldilocks' zone'? Where are the high prior attainers – what's the same, what's different? Where are the low prior attainers? Where are the SEND pupils?
	Do pupils express what they are doing, why and how it builds on from what they did yesterday, last week, last year …?
Meeting with pupils (those observed in lessons) with their books: approximately 30 minutes.	Broad questions that check whether the pedagogy and curriculum presented by the leader translates to knowledge, skills and understanding in the pupils.
	Look at their books – what was this work? What did you learn? What did you need to know beforehand? How will it help with what you are doing now? Where do you think it will go next?
	Can't add much here. Our pupils are lovely but at times too passive – their attitudes to learning were (in the majority) not quite where we would want them to be, according to the grade descriptors.
Work scrutiny from a range of year groups and key stages (with subject leader): approximately 30 minutes.	What does the vision and methodology you discussed at the start of the deep dive look like in the books?
	Can you exemplify where it is working well?
	Can you exemplify how CPD has improved it and where it isn't working well?
	Have you identified, before you even look, which teachers, books and lessons were going to be better or needing improvement?

Teacher interviews.	Why did you teach what you taught? Where does it come from (they can't just say 'medium-term plans')? Adapting for needs of pupils but always with the aim of achieving age-related expectations or the rapid closing of gaps.

Other areas

■ Behaviour and attitudes: like deep dive – policy, paperwork and detail then tested at class, pupil and adult level.

■ Safeguarding: after SCR, it's DSL and key records, processes and so on, but don't forget preventative rather than reactive policies, and don't forget site safety and risk assessments (paper and dynamic). A few easily reached examples will make your words look solid but, as above, they will be tested with parents, pupils and staff.

■ Pupil premium: not much changed – challenges around data if there is a difference. Precision of spend is key.

Attendance was interesting: our persistent absence has come down from 15.3% to 9.3% – still above the national average, but in reality only out by three pupils.

Note: There is behaviour and conduct and then there is learning behaviours – make sure both layers are good. The wider curriculum is key.

(*This was a good inspection, helped by very thorough preparation, and I'm very grateful for this amount of detail. Thank you to my writer!*)

These eight examples show the range of different experiences. The main message is: be prepared for anything. Your inspector may be on your side, or not, but thorough preparation is key. This last head teacher, other heads and some of the subject leaders too did exactly that.

EPILOGUE

Well, there you are. Another Ofsted framework and one that is very different from any that have gone before. I hope you have found the inspection advice – from preparation beforehand to inspection methodology, SEF writing and the experiences of the EIF from people in schools – to have been useful. Of course, the COVID-19 outbreak and associated school closures alter the timetable of inspection and may even alter its focus, but the likelihood is that Ofsted will be back, strengthened by extra HMI to support the inspection of outstanding schools, after it is over.

I can't stress enough the importance of good preparation, so please ignore Ofsted's advice not to prepare for your inspection. That advice is there in order for Ofsted to control you and the process. Instead, *take control* yourself and, by doing so, create the edge that you need in order to persuade a lead inspector that what you see in your school is what Ofsted should see in your school.

You have two days and a 90-minute phone call to do just that. Good luck, but I hope you are well prepared enough not to need it!

APPENDICES: PRIMARY AND SECONDARY SEF WRITING TOOLS

PRIMARY SELF-EVALUATION TOOL

How to write your SEF

(Applicable to junior, middle and infant schools.)

A self-evaluation has only one purpose: to put an idea of the grade you think you deserve in your lead inspector's head. The length of your self-evaluation form (SEF) doesn't matter as much as the telling of a persuasive story.

Don't combine your SEF with your school development plan (SDP). The audience and purpose is very different, and the SDP will hand your lead inspector his or her inspection trails on a plate.

Make sure you have the EIF 2019 section 5 handbook with you as you write.

Start your SEF with a clear indication of where you judge your school to be, set out in a separate sentence – for example, 'We believe that X School is a good school.' The rest of your SEF then forms a document to back up that statement. Really, writing an SEF is as easy as that. Then follow the Ofsted handbook areas.

For me, it's about clarity of purpose, and too many schools write an SEF without a clear purpose. In consequence, they include where they are successful but they also expose every weakness under headings such as 'what we need to do to improve'. It can then effectively become a series of inspection trails for your lead inspector and can be evidence that you are not doing things well enough. The SEF should also be written in proud and confident language. It is a document of information but also of persuasion. Wherever you can, illustrate it with positives from your last inspection.

Begin with your school's context, but also make this your Ofsted context, and then include information about your school. You then need a section on information about your school and one on your progress in meeting the issues from your previous inspection, before embarking on an explanation of the main SEF areas.

Context

Context is the second most important section of your SEF after quality of education. This will be the first sight your lead inspector has of your own picture of the school. Briefly detail the intent and implementation of your school's curriculum. Also detail the main points of your published data and how much extra your pupils learn because of the cogency of your curriculum (your impact). State how you believe pupils are progressing in the current school year too. Although the team shouldn't ask for internal tracking data, there is no harm in directing them to the quality of what they will see in class, in books and in talking to all stakeholders, via a statement about how well current pupils are performing across the school (not just in Year 6). Link this to the quality of your curriculum.

In a separate paragraph, describe the level of skills that children bring on entry to the school and the progress they make from their starting points. It is very important to establish children's skills on entry with a clarity that is persuasive (see more below), so introduce this now. A sentence to play about with could be: 'Our pupils join with skills well below those of other pupils nationally, and they make progress across the school because of our excellent curriculum provision and good teaching to achieve outcomes approaching national norms on leaving.'

In a school facing challenging circumstances, for which value-added published data can be difficult, this can be an impact lifesaver, if you can persuade your lead inspector that it is true. On inspection, progress does not begin from the attainment on entry of pupils to Key Stage 2, unless you are a junior school. It begins from pupils' starting points when they joined the school. In an infant school, the establishment of these starting points is absolutely crucial, as there are no national progress measures. The explanation of progress is in your hands. In your quality of education section and during your inspection, expand this explanation and make these baselines effectively unchallengeable. The impact that leaders and managers have on pupils is a very clear expectation (para. 225, p. 61, S5). It is telling that the introduction to the leadership and management judgements does not talk about curriculum at all, but about impact (para. 228, p. 64, S5).

Set out your vision here. Do it succinctly and explain how this is communicated to all staff. If you have a vision statement, include it and make it clear. If you wish to play the game and include curriculum somewhere in that vision, so be it, but all stakeholders need to reflect the school's vision to inspectors, so make the message simple.

Use the context statement to bring up the main strengths in each area early, with a brief introduction to all five judgement areas and your judgement grades. You might also wish to state that you have improved considerably from the last inspection, anticipating that section. Be brief, but mention the main strengths in your curriculum and ensure that you elucidate your curriculum intent and how this looks in practice (implementation). Mention how this has helped reading and mathematical knowledge (impact criteria, p. 51, S5). Mention strengths under safeguarding, governance and spiritual, moral, social and cultural development (SMSC), so they are in the mind of your reader before they get to these sections later.

To repeat: this is your first chance to give a very clear initial statement of skills on entry to reception and nursery (if you have one), and make it clear that progress across your nursery boosts your reception baseline scores via the children that transfer. *Paint this picture as low as you can evidence.* This is the single most important thing you will do in the whole of your primary SEF. Don't lie, don't make it unbelievable, but don't be conservative about your skills on entry. This gives the basis for progress across the whole school. The details can come in under 'quality of education' later. Mention the effect of transience, especially if any outliers have seriously affected your progress and attainment in Analyse School Performance (ASP). Use proud language throughout. This is your school and let that show.

Infant schools

Progress is in your hands. There are no national measures, so you have to build a picture using on-entry data (don't ignore transience and lower skills special educational needs and disability (SEND) outliers) and your Key Stage 1 data. Now that curriculum rules, this should be a boon to you.

Junior schools

Hopefully, Ofsted's promises about looking at curriculum first will produce a very different slant to inspection for you, away from data which is often flawed. Let's wait and see. I would still be wary and focus on that data, as well as curriculum. The same advice from the previous framework holds true: create your own baselines from your Key Stage 2 entrants or you could be hamstrung by data from your feeder infant schools. This is difficult, as you know, but use the impact part of the 'quality of education' section in your SEF to set out your arguments and stick with them. Inspectors are expected to look carefully at on-entry and progress data for junior schools (para. 308, p. 90, S5). Get the inspection team on your side from the start with a persuasive iteration of your own progress arguments, perhaps setting aside the inspection data summary report (IDSR) as inaccurate.

Information about this school

The 'information about this school' section from the previous inspection report (updated using the context page in IDSR) will give you much of the other contextual information you need. However, flesh out the deprivation in your catchment with local authority and Income Deprivation Affecting Children Index (IDACI) data.

Progress in meeting the previous Ofsted inspection key issues

Include a separate section on progress in meeting previous inspection issues to alert your inspectors to the fact that you have addressed these and that progress has been made. Use subheadings for each one.

Main SEF areas

There are five sections in the new inspection framework: quality of education, behaviour and attitudes, personal development, leadership and management, and early years education. Work using the EIF 2019 section 5 handbook as a guide. The section 8 handbook will inform your inspection if you are a good or outstanding school, but it doesn't include any grade descriptors and you will need these when writing your SEF. You will not be awarded grades, but will instead get an inspection letter from your section 8 inspection team with the three outcomes (para. 72, p. 18, S8). Choose the grade descriptor that reflects your judgement and evidence all the sentences in that judgement grade throughout. Make it clear that there are areas where you feel things are better than in the grade descriptor. Don't flag up areas where you feel progress is not as good (unless you couch the negative in a positive) and don't use language that would direct a lead inspector to an evidence trail that wouldn't be helpful to you.

Organise your self-evaluation to reflect the judgement order of the EIF 2019 handbook. However, although curriculum, via quality of education, has clearly risen up the order of importance, in my opinion your published outcomes will remain a key judgement in the eyes of your lead inspector. My advice here is not to fully believe Ofsted that curriculum will dominate your lead inspector's thinking until this is clearly shown to be the case (although it *may* dominate the on-the-ground inspection techniques and it *may* provide you with an escape route from results that don't look great) and to make the impact of your curriculum on your results thoroughly persuasive, through carefully explaining your pupil outcomes.

Quality of education

Quality of education is by far the most important section for your next inspection. Make no mistake, Ofsted are looking for a particular approach with regard to curriculum intent and implementation – impact remains similar – so organise your SEF accordingly, with three separate subheadings, and play their game. In my opinion, it is too much of a risk, unless your data is stone-cold excellent, to do otherwise, and I truly wish I didn't have to write that. The language you use is important, so I would write your SEF and construct your arguments carefully, reflecting Ofsted's own language at apposite times.

Intent

Make your intent proud and personal and ensure that the strapline, at least, is known by all stakeholders. You have your own context, so the intent of your curriculum may be different to that of other schools (para. 175, p. 42, S5). It should be bespoke to you: what is in your curriculum that is unique to your school? How have you designed your curriculum to reflect this?

The handbook (para. 179, p. 43, S5) says that 'inspectors will draw evidence about leaders' curriculum "intent" principally from discussions with senior and subject leaders', and the bullets in this paragraph give you the specific information to include and explain in your section on curriculum intent. In terms of preparation, there is likely to be a much greater burden on middle leaders in subject deep dives. Ensure they are fully briefed on the school's curriculum intent and how the curriculum intent is then sequenced in their own subject to enhance pupils' knowledge. I fully understand the difficulties of subject leadership in the foundation subjects in primary schools, especially small ones, but this is something that heads are going to have to plan for on inspection. In addition, state that you quality assure your curriculum intent through regular meetings; the need for quality assurance was stressed to inspectors in July 2019 EIF training.

Implementation

Ofsted say (para. 182, p. 44, S5) that 'inspectors will primarily evaluate how the curriculum is taught at subject and classroom level'. The bullets in the next paragraph set out what they will be looking for and therefore what to explain in this section. Ofsted believe that learning can be defined as 'an alteration in long-term memory and not just memorising disconnected facts' (para. 184, p. 45, S5). Show how your improving outcomes are illustrating that this is true, or how your intent and implementation are so well structured that it is clear that pupil outcomes will respond over time. Ofsted assert that they will take account of the fact that curriculum redesign will take time to impact on results, especially in schools in challenging circumstances. (I know – let's hope they actually do!)

I'm sure you have noticed that there is no judgement any more for quality of teaching. Instead, it is in the implementation section where you must link teaching quality to curriculum intent and to impact (results). Look at the grade descriptors at the end of this section under 'implementation' (pp. 50–51, S5). It's all about the work of teachers. Explain how their work leads to your results in this section. Use the grade descriptor bullets to help you. It is also worth explaining your reading policy at this stage, together with your phonics planning and provision, and mesh these with your curriculum, as three of the criteria for implementation mention either reading or phonics (the other seven are about teaching).

I will deal with the use of internal assessment data here, but it crops up in both intent and impact. Ofsted are clear that 'Inspectors will not look at non-statutory internal progress and attainment data on section 5 and section 8 inspections of schools' (para. 194, p. 47, S5). However, other paragraphs describe the school's use of assessment, always stepping carefully around their original statement about not asking for data. How inspectors can 'evaluate how assessment is used in the school to support the teaching of the curriculum' (para. 186, p. 45, S5) without looking at current internal data is a mystery. It's a contradiction that, I think, allows you to still use internal assessment data with inspectors, although some will say, 'No, I'm not looking.' Please accept this if they do, but qualify it with something like, 'I'm sure you'll see, in everything we do, that our internal data accurately reflects where we think we are.' Don't let them off the hook if you know your improvement is rapid but is not yet reflected in published results. Direct them to the excellence of your curriculum intent and implementation to support this.

If you feel that your internal assessment procedures give you a good handle on how much progress your pupils are making *and* you can demonstrate accuracy in predictions in previous years, include this data in your SEF, under 'impact', and explain their use, but be mindful of Ofsted's attempts to reduce workload. Be especially mindful of para. 189, p. 45, S5. If Ofsted feel your assessment procedures are work-heavy and your published data is making your lead inspector twitchy, you can bet that he or she will use your assessment procedures as a stick to beat you with, which may result in a letter stating that they will return for a section 5 inspection within one to two years (outcome 3, para. 72, p. 18, S8). If your data is pretty good, the same procedures will probably attract no more than a comment in a 'continuing good' report (outcome 1, para. 72, p. 18, S8). Tread carefully. There is no need to give Ofsted that stick, and unless these issues arise during your inspection you could keep your procedures under the table and deal with them only if that can of worms is opened. Two or three data collection points is what Ofsted are expecting, no more (para. 188, p. 45, S5).

Ofsted describe how they will collect this evidence (para. 189, p. 46, S5), and this can be used in conjunction with, or instead of, internal assessment data to show how you are implementing your curriculum.

Impact

Impact is probably the area of quality of education with which school leaders will be most familiar. It is effectively the old 'pupil outcomes' section of the 2015–2018 framework, combined with how much extra knowledge they have gained. When Ofsted refer to 'what pupils have learned' (para. 192, p. 46, S5), they mean what published results they have gained (or what your internal data is showing, if you can get your inspector to listen).

Ofsted believe that 'all learning builds towards an end point' (para. 193, p. 47, S5) and information sessions about EIF 2019 have indicated that it is up to schools what that end point is. However, the handbook is clear (para. 197, p. 48, S5): national assessments and examinations are your end points – that is, the end of early years, Key Stage 1 and Key Stage 2, with the Year 1 phonics screening check and Year 2 resits as staging points. It is particularly important to highlight results in reading in your SEF, and therefore how you integrate and organise the promotion of reading in the curriculum. All stakeholders, especially subject leaders, should be able to talk about how their subject helps pupils to read, and read widely, throughout their time with you.

Aim to organise your impact section along those lines, with these areas as subheadings. If you wish to write about the impact of early years separately, you can, but add an overarching, 'Our pupils start [here] at the beginning of nursery/reception and get to [here] at the end of Year 6' (as you have said in your context statement) to allow a smooth progression of explanation.

Structuring impact

Include a short opening context statement in which you state how you can see that pupils' knowledge and skills have moved on, via your improving results, at early years foundation stage, Key Stage 1 and Key Stage 2 in attainment and progress. If these results are not there yet, point again to the excellence of your curriculum intent and implementation and state that you are certain this will have a significant future impact. Repeat the language you have used about skills on entry here and use that to judge progress across the whole school. Try to make progress across key stages and across subjects and pupil groups as level as possible. If one group is making less than expected progress it can open a huge can of very poisonous worms, so this needs cautious explanation! Explain any possible areas of weakness carefully. There will be a story to tell. Data is key (Ofsted now call data 'performance information' (para. 197, p. 48, S5)). Pack this section full of data and show that you have an excellent grasp of it. Tables are good, but explain each table you include in an accompanying commentary.

Don't be afraid to use other data, over and above your IDSR. Your inspectors will not have seen, say, Fischer Family Trust (FFT) data or progress data from other commercial packages. Use whatever data you can to supplement, or even contradict, ASP data. Use positive pupil/parent comments and questionnaire data to back up your judgement.

Possible grade 2 lifelines

■ **Transience (stability).** Be very clear on how transience in and through a key stage may have affected your data, and also how transience out (easily forgotten) of higher ability pupils has possibly affected your data (if it has). Next to attainment on entry, high transience can be the key to explaining why progress, and especially attainment, may not be showing correctly in your IDSR. It may just provide you with a lifeline.

■ **Outliers.** The effects of outliers, which can be seen in your IDSR scatterplots, can be a possible second grade 2 lifeline. ASP does now exclude the most obvious outliers, but you may have a rash of them in one cohort. I hope your lead inspector understands the effect that outliers – which may lie beyond your control – could have on your progress and attainment data. If they don't, you must tell them! By outliers, I mean the lowest-performing pupils in your attainment and progress IDSR scatterplots.

■ **Explain the progress of your current pupils fully.** Even though Ofsted state that inspectors won't consider this data. Data may not be just improving in the current Year 6 and Year 2, but improvements may be clear in other year groups, and progress may already have been accelerating in those year groups during the previous year. If this is the case, your team needs to know this.

Stress these as yet unseen (to your inspectors, through their data) improvements and clearly explain the links to improving curriculum and the quality of leadership and teaching. Tables could be prepared that can be updated easily with your latest data drop straight after the inspection phone call. If you can persuade your inspection team that a corner has already been turned in pupil progress, you may have a vital way into persuading your lead inspector that your school is improving or that last year's Year 6 and Year 2 data is not the start of a declining trend. On inspection, Ofsted state this will be seen in books, talking to leaders at all levels and especially to pupils about how much extra they know. Thus, Ofsted can leave you alone for at least another three years as a school that continues to be good.

When writing your impact section, follow this pattern of subheadings and information:

1. **Key Stage 2 attainment on entry, attainment and then progress.** Start with a short context summary statement, then add more context/commentary, fully explaining any apparent weaknesses but also highlighting strengths.

2. **Key Stage 1 attainment on entry, attainment and then progress**. Again, start with a short context summary statement, then add more context/commentary, fully explaining any apparent weaknesses but also highlighting strengths. In comparison to other schools, your IDSR contains no progress measures from early years to the end of Key Stage 1, only the numbers of pupils who achieve expected progress, or above or below expected progress, in your school. This can leave a primary school which takes from a very deprived and low-ability catchment looking rather exposed at Key Stage 1. However, your intake may, typically, include a large number of pupils whose cognitive abilities are lower than other pupils nationally. It is harder for them to make the predicted progress and they are not expected to have caught up until the end of Year 6. If your Key Stage 2 outcomes are better than your Key Stage 1 outcomes and you are laying the foundations for that whole-school progress in the younger years, argue that there is time for them to continue their catching up. If some pupils' cognitive abilities are such that they are unlikely ever to rise above low in a cohort, explain this to your inspectors via your SEF, but hopefully they will already have been removed from your attainment and progress scores. Check, disaggregate and recalculate if this is the case. In a class of 30, two pupils make up a whopping 7% of your data.

3. **Phonics screening check.** Explain your results over time, explaining apparent weaknesses but highlighting strengths. Suggest how strong progress has been from starting points to the Year 1 phonics check (there is no IDSR measure, of course). If your reception data shows significant weaknesses in communication, language and literacy, then phonics check outcomes that are still below average in Year 1 may still point to very good progress from low starting points.

4. **Early years.** I would recommend including your early years data here (not in your 'quality of early years' section) because it ties early years into overall school progress better, but it is up to you. Make your case for skills on entry carefully and confidently using the last Ofsted report's comments on attainment on entry as a guide (if they said your pupils come in with skills on entry 'well-below

those expected for their age' or even 'low', that could be gold dust!). But bear in mind that things may have changed from that inspection and skills on entry may have fallen. If they have, evidence it. Remember that entry data for this particular academic year may well not reflect the entry data of the current Year 6 cohort or the cohort that has just left (which forms your IDSR), so dig back for these data and include them. It will be foundation stage profile exit data from seven years ago. This can make for good and believable comparisons. Include good level of development (GLD) data for the last few years – from your entry data to your GLD exit data you have your progress across early years.

I know I'm banging on about this, but don't over-egg any recent on-entry baseline assessments because the Department for Education/ Ofsted may use your baselines in seven years' time as measures from which to judge progress across the school, although recent confusion and a Department for Education change of mind around baselines have rendered recent data very questionable. That gives you a good lever to introduce your own assessment data and to present this as more robust and cogent than any baseline data you may have collected for an outside provider. Talk them down!

Have a weight of evidence to justify your assessments, including any moderation data that supports you. Don't be tempted to be expansive with GLD exit data: you could leave Key Stage 1 in difficulties when showing progress. Think of a nice, rising straight line for progress across the school, not a line with flats and curves in it!

If you have a nursery, organise your data in the same way: entry assessments to exit data. Don't exaggerate your entry data for children joining reception, but ensure that it shows progress across nursery.

Explain Key Stage 2 data first, as it has a much higher weighting in the eyes of the inspection team: it is the end of statutory education in primary school. These all have to be consistent – for example, attainment at Key Stage 1 is unlikely to be average if attainment on entry to Key Stage 2 is below average. Progress across Key Stage 2 can't be good if attainment on entry into Year 3 is average and attainment in Year 6 is average.

Within Key Stage 1 and Key Stage 2, progress in English, maths and all the various groups need to be covered: SEND, free school meals, English as an additional language/ethnic minorities, boys/girls, low/medium/higher attaining pupils. Be especially clear about the progress of disadvantaged pupils, disadvantaged most able pupils and the progress of the most able pupils (a continuing Ofsted focus and mentioned many times in EIF 2019). It is now not so much about whether you are narrowing the gap with non-disadvantaged pupils during their time in your school, it is whether you are narrowing the gap with all other pupils nationally. Explain fully why this may not have happened in the past and use current data as well as you can to explain why this is changing. If the progress of a particular group appears to be slowing and especially if it is the progress of a disadvantaged group, that can spell trouble. Use your current year's data to show the trend is reversing. A picture of a few differences in rates of progress, or even improvements in rates of progress over time, against each group's respective national figures, would be ideal.

Any difficulties or inconsistencies between groups should be explained. If there is standout poor progress of one group, address the reasons with that group's data, and don't forget the importance of data from current pupils. Don't miss the positives: the 'standout' may be some groups who are doing particularly well!

Don't overlook 'learning well across the curriculum' because here is where you can evidence how you achieve this in numeracy, and especially literacy, by employing other subjects to help. This is likely to be explored in any deep dive into a subject. How individual subjects help all pupils to read widely will be questioned. And don't miss explaining clearly how you ensure your pupils learn how to read well and how you have embedded synthetic phonics. Provide data here on the progress of interventions such as reading schemes as evidence that any pupils who may be at risk of falling behind are supported.

Use pupil/parent comments, any outside survey information (e.g. Kirkland Rowell) and questionnaire data to back up your judgement.

Don't forget to look over the grade descriptors (pp. 49–52, S5), checking that you have included information in your 'quality of education' section which would support the bullets relevant to the grade you want.

It is a best fit, but that does leave it up to your inspectors and especially your lead inspector. Persuade them!

Behaviour and attitudes

The first paragraph in this section (para. 201, p. 52, S5) gives you your reason for writing this section. It is about how you create a safe, calm, orderly and positive environment, so that is what you must evidence. The bullet points in the next paragraph list all the areas you must cover.

Start by judging where you feel behaviour and attitudes is in your school and use the whole section to back up that judgement with quantitative evidence. 'No statement without evidence to back it up' should be your mantra. If you say that continuing professional development has happened, justify with quantitative, monitored evidence that it has had an impact in the classroom. Use specific examples to illustrate and link to outcome data from the 'quality of education' section above.

Paragraphs 205–207 (pp. 53–54, S5) about school culture and sanctions, especially around exclusions (which have risen up the Ofsted agenda), are important. Highlight and explain your procedures and outcomes. Link low exclusions to excellent safeguarding and inclusion. As before, inspectors will choose some SEND case studies to look at, so say that these case studies are robust, secure and helpful to you. Don't miss paragraph 208 (p. 54, S5) on alternative strategies to exclusion: for an inclusive school, this is a good invitation to set out what you do.

Your attendance data over time goes in this section. This needs to show that it is above the lowest 10% nationally and is improving over time. Use whatever you can to show this improvement in the current year group. Disaggregate pupils who have left but who are still counting, pupils who are/were on your books for a time but who never arrived, school closures for illness outbreaks, snow days, pupils who have had a severe illness and needed a long time for recovery – whatever you can to show an improvement from the previous year's figures. Few lead inspectors will wish to hang a school on attendance if it is clearly doing well overall. As such, they will value your explanations to get them out of a potential hole with the HMI who does the quality assurance on their evidence base and report. If attendance is improving, link this to increased engagement through the improving curriculum.

Paragraph 213 and its attendant bullets explain how Ofsted will inspect behaviour and attitudes. Ensure you are fine with these points. There is no need to write about all of them, but elaborate on any issues where the information could be wobbly.

Don't forget to look over the grade descriptors (pp. 57–58, S5), checking that you have included information in your behaviour and attitudes section which would support the bullets relevant to the grade you want. It is a best fit, but that does leave it up to your inspectors and especially your lead inspector. Persuade them!

Personal development

In the EIF, personal development is now separate to behaviour (this used to be 'personal development, behaviour and welfare'). The separation actually gives behaviour and attitudes and personal development a more prominent place in the inspection team's thinking.

Paragraphs 216–217 (p. 58, S5) provide the rationale behind this grade. Intent, implementation and impact are all there, as this is effectively another curriculum section – this time, the wider curriculum (including SMSC) which supports pupils' personal development. It would be well worth organising this section along the lines of the new Ofsted constructs, but it's up to you. Just ensure you mention them, perhaps quite often!

Paragraph 218 (pp. 58–59, S5) outlines all the things you need to evidence in your SEF. Make sure you describe each one, although many could be combined. There is no need for a subheading for each, unless you really wish to do so.

Spiritual, moral, social and cultural development

There are no judgement criteria for SMSC development and it is not judged separately. In many ways, SMSC has been reduced in importance in this framework and inadequate SMSC will no longer lead to grade 4. SMSC has been included in personal development, instead of under overall effectiveness, as it was previously. Still, it is worth giving it its own section.

What is expected of you is clearly set out in paragraphs 219–223 (pp. 59–60, S5), so use subheadings for all four areas and write this according to the bullet points on those pages. There is a great deal of overlap with the promotion of equality of opportunity, the protection of pupils from radicalisation and extremism, and the promotion of traditional British values, which all fall within leadership and management in the handbook. There is nothing wrong with covering all those issues here. It would save duplication.

Keep the focus on quantitative evidence and pupil/parent comments – you can use those on Parent View. Any outside survey information (e.g. Kirkland Rowell) or questionnaire data can help here too. In addition, link social and moral education to behaviour and attitudes outcomes wherever you can.

Don't forget to look over the grade descriptors (pp. 62–64, S5), checking that you have included information in your personal development section which would support the bullets relevant to the grade you want. It is a best fit, but that does leave it up to your inspectors and especially your lead inspector. Persuade them!

Leadership and management

Begin by judging the effectiveness of leadership and management in your school and use the whole section to back up that judgement with as much quantitative evidence as you can. Link it especially to pupil outcomes and curriculum improvements.

Don't be afraid to talk highly of the head teacher here, even if you are writing the section yourself, as the head teacher! You are a crucial part of leadership and management. Use comments from others to do this. Leadership starts with the head teacher or principal, but it needs to be evidenced at all levels.

Paragraph 229 (p. 64, S5) gives you the rationale behind Ofsted's intent – and note their inclusion of the word 'research' in this statement. Play the game in this section and drop in references to the research behind your decisions, especially about curriculum.

The succeeding eight bullets set out the areas you need to write about and evidence.

If you are a part of a multi-academy trust (MAT), the roles and responsibilities of the school within the MAT need to be explained (paras 233–235, p. 65, S5). If you are not, ignore these. This could be done at the start of the next section on governance.

Let each sentence in the handbook's grade descriptors (pp. 74–75, S5) guide you, so you don't leave out things like governors, parents, safeguarding and especially how leaders have conceived and implemented a curriculum bespoke to your school.

There is tangential reference to partnerships in the descriptors, via a mention of trustees if you are in a MAT, but paragraphs 245 and 246 (p. 67, S5) reference partnerships more explicitly, so include it in your writing. If the use of external agencies has been used appropriately and successfully in particular areas (e.g. teaching, behaviour, SMSC), reference this in the individual section, referring to evidence of improvement. Seeking help should not be regarded as weakness; this is about seeking particular expertise that you may not have in the school and can be presented as a positive for leadership and management.

The rest of the leadership and management section is a series of subheadings to evidence the areas to which the handbook gives particular importance. All are included in the inadequate descriptors (p. 75, S5) and are limiting judgements for your grade. That is, fail *any* of these and you will be judged inadequate for leadership and management, and thus grade 4 overall. The following points need to be explained separately:

■ Governance.

■ Use of the pupil premium and its effectiveness.

■ Gaming.

■ Inclusion and off-rolling.

■ Safeguarding.

Governance

If you are in a MAT, paragraphs 238 and 239 (p. 66, S5) describe how roles and responsibilities should be explained. Don't leave this until the day of inspection for your governors/trustees to explain, although it will be in the lead inspector's checklist to discuss in the 90-minute pre-inspection phone call. Explain your governance structure fully here. If you are not in a MAT, ignore this; your governing body is the responsible body.

Paragraphs 241–243 (pp. 66–67, S5) set out the areas around which Ofsted will ask questions to governors. They stress the importance of the *Governance Handbook* more in this framework,[1] so any inspection governance team must show that they have knowledge of its contents. A knowledge of intent and implementation of the curriculum is also necessary. Ensure that your SEF communicates your confidence in your governing body/trustees and that their knowledge is good. If that confidence proves weak, it will leave you vulnerable to requires improvement/special measures.

A note to your governors here: don't be blindsided by focusing completely on intent and implementation of the curriculum; impact is still important. When asked about this, be prepared to explain the school's results and say how any improvements are related to curriculum and other factors. If improvements are rapid, but are not yet showing fully in published data, don't be afraid to refer to internal data to demonstrate this. Also be prepared to accept an inspector saying that they can't look at it, but counter with, 'Just look at the evidence in classrooms, teaching, books and the ethos and positive learning environment in the school. You can't miss it and we know this through our monitoring.' Something similar could go in the 'quality of education' section of the SEF. Take control, leaders and governors!

Use of the pupil premium

Paragraph 244 (p. 67, S5) outlines your writing points on the pupil premium. Refer to the information on your website for much of this – there

---

1   Department for Education, *Governance Handbook for Academies, Multi-Academy Trusts and Maintained Schools* (March 2019). Available at: https://www.gov.uk/government/publications/governance-handbook.

is no need to repeat it. Use this section to link your curriculum intent to your rationale for spending the pupil premium and to your results.

Off-site provision

If you use no off-site provision, say so. If you do, paragraphs 247–253 (pp. 67–68, S5) apply. This has been expanded greatly from the previous framework, with inspectors being asked to investigate the use of off-site provision carefully. This is due to Ofsted's focus on unregistered schools, especially those of a religious nature; Ofsted now have a dedicated unregistered schools team. Explain carefully and ensure you know about the registration status of any alternative providers that you use. Paragraph 252 explains the consequences! It is down to you to check, and if Ofsted get a sniff of the use of an unregistered school for alternative provision, the consequence may well be special measures.

Gaming

Gaming is new to this framework and is explained in paragraph 254 (p. 68, S5). It is well worthwhile including a short paragraph explaining why your curriculum and exam entries should not, in any way, come under the label of 'gaming the system'.

Inclusion and off-rolling

Inclusion and off-rolling are also new to this framework. If this doesn't apply to your school, say exactly that. Hopefully, it doesn't apply to you, but if you are off-rolling pupils the consequences are special measures (and should be, in my opinion). Have a read of paragraphs 256–261 (pp. 69–70, S5) and be aware of your responsibilities.

Safeguarding

Safeguarding is a big part of inspection and it is something you simply must get right for your pupils. However, there is a recognition at Ofsted that safeguarding has improved and it may not feel to you that the inspection team's focus is as strong as it used to be. 'Don't open cans of worms' is the overriding maxim here. However, if you have an ongoing safeguarding worry, explain it fully.

Ofsted instruct their inspectors to be familiar with two pieces of statutory guidance in relation to safeguarding, so you should be familiar with them too. I'm sure you know them already. The first is *Keeping Children Safe in Education: Statutory Guidance for Schools and Colleges*[2] and the second is *Working Together to Safeguard Children*.[3] There are also three other 'guides for inspection' listed in the footer on p. 71 (S5) (one is a duplication). These tell inspectors what they must do and how they must do it, so it may be worth knowing their contents.

To go through the intricacies of safeguarding is too big a scope for this SEF tool, or for your SEF, but if you get safeguarding wrong on a daily basis, beyond simple administrative errors which can easily be corrected on inspection, you are not doing right by the pupils in your school, and lead inspectors and inspection teams will not be kind. Nor should they be. Write safeguarding as strong, unless it really isn't; but if it isn't, you are very likely to be looking at grade 4 for leadership and management and for overall effectiveness.

It is worth mentioning your website here and whether it is compliant. Your lead inspector has to state whether it is or is not compliant. To do that, of course, you must ensure that it is![4] Follow the link for 'advice on publishing information about your school's governors' because buried in this document is what you should publish on your website regarding governors' interests.[5] If your website is not compliant, because of a particular and valid reason, say so; don't be found out.

In addition, to help your lead inspector, you could add a sentence like this (or copy it, providing it's true): 'There is no negative information, safeguarding or otherwise, of which we are aware, on the Internet or in

2   Department for Education, *Keeping Children Safe in Education: Statutory Guidance for Schools and Colleges* (September 2019). Available at: https://www.gov.uk/government/publications/keeping-children-safe-in-education--2.

3   Department for Education, *Working Together to Safeguard Children: A Guide to Inter-Agency Working to Safeguard and Promote the Welfare of Children* (July 2018). Available at: https://www.gov.uk/government/publications/working-together-to-safeguard-children--2.

4   All the information that maintained schools should put on their website can be found at: https://www.gov.uk/guidance/what-maintained-schools-must-publish-online.

5   Department for Education, *The Constitution of Governing Bodies of Maintained Schools: Statutory Guidance for Governing Bodies of Maintained Schools and Local Authorities in England* (August 2017), pp. 11–12. Available at: https://www.gov.uk/government/publications/constitution-of-governing-bodies-of-maintained-schools.

the local press from the local authority, Department for Education or police concerning our pupils.'

Paragraphs 262–272 (pp. 71–72, S5) give you all the information you need to structure your safeguarding section. Your SCR will be checked. Paragraphs 44 and 53 imply this, although there is no specific mention of it in leadership and management. Make sure that it is up to date, has no gaps (that is what they will scan for) and you can justify the evidence trails that sit behind the content, and say all of this in your SEF.

The quality of early years education

This section is judged separately, as before. Give one grade overall; there is no need to give grades for each area. However, you may wish to follow the requirements of report writing by giving a written grade for each area – for example, 'Leadership and management of early years is outstanding because ...' Your lead inspector will be expected to do this when they write their report.

Early years will only get a short paragraph in the report, at best. In some, it is not mentioned specifically but is subsumed into the overall report. Word counts are strict.

Organise your early years section into the following areas:

■ Context.

■ Quality of education.

■ Behaviour and attitudes.

■ Personal development.

■ Leadership and management.

The bullets in paragraph 279 (p. 77, S5) give you the areas on which to focus in your writing, but I would use the structure above to organise this section.

Context

Set out the context of your early years in a short statement. State whether you have a nursery and how many children transfer to reception or from how many other nurseries your children come. Mention, again, skills on entry and don't be conservative. *Paint these as low as you can.* If children who join your reception are joined by others from different nurseries, explain how many join and especially highlight if you can show that *your* children join with better skills because of the quality of provision in your nursery. Mention any recent building work or changes in provision since your last inspection.

Quality of education in the early years

Within quality of education (paras 279–289, pp. 77–82, S5), curriculum intent and implementation are important, but I believe that the impact of early years will still have a pull on your inspectors' minds, so make sure this is explained well in your main 'quality of education' section. It's good that the third bullet point (para. 282, p. 77, S5) contains the word 'progress', which you can evidence, as there is (as yet) no national measure or comparator. But the pupils' 'readiness for the next stage in their education' is a worry, as it implies attainment and thus a percentage of GLDs.

If you are a school in challenging circumstances and take many pupils whose skills on entry are far below what may be expected for their age, evidence this and state that there is no expectation that these pupils should be at national levels of attainment until Year 6, at least. Consequently, progress must be the judge of your effectiveness. Be clear on this and don't let the imperative go. If your inspector wants to focus on percentage of GLDs, call the Ofsted helpline and complain there and then. Don't leave it until after the inspection.

It is quite possible, as I have said, for you to explain your early years impact in your main 'quality of education' section. It's up to you, but I would recommend describing it there.

Paragraph 287 (p. 78, S5) will help you to include what is relevant to inspectors. It refers to a 'logical progression' in the early years curriculum (second bullet) and it is about 'content, sequencing and progression in all seven areas of learning in EYFS'. It mentions developing, consolidating and deepening pupils' knowledge. Ignore these at your peril! Ofsted have got the traditional, knowledge-based curriculum bit between their teeth, even in early years. They also expect to see a curriculum bespoke to your setting and context. Progress is the key. If you can persuade them that your children make good progress, they are more likely to say that your curriculum supports this than if they feel progress is weak.

Behaviour and attitudes in the early years

Apply similar writing criteria to the main behaviour and attitudes section, but this doesn't have to be a long section. Be positive about how well your children settle in and, hopefully, the inspectors will see that.

Personal development in the early years

Children's personal, social and emotional development are explicitly referenced in the fourth bullet point of paragraph 282 (p. 77, S5). It's worth using this as a basis for writing this section. In addition, mirror what you have written in your main personal development section earlier.

Leadership and management in the early years

Link the effectiveness of leadership and management in early years to your outcomes and especially to progress. Explain how leaders have carefully designed a curriculum to focus on the needs of your children and on progression through the seven areas of learning. Paragraph 286 (p. 78, S5) asks you to describe care before/after school and in school holidays, so do so, and explain the need (intent), hours and provision in, say, your breakfast club. If you have provision for 2- and 3-year-olds, paragraph 288 (p. 78, S5) helps you to write about it. Mention early reading, early mathematics and phonics (para. 287, p. 78, S5 and the descriptors), how this is organised and how effective the teaching is of both.

Familiarise yourself with the grade descriptors at the end of the section (pp. 79–82, S5). These will help you to cover all areas around which you will be inspected.

Paragraph 281 (p. 77, S5) makes it clear that the effectiveness of the arrangements for safeguarding children in early years is reflected in the main judgement for the school. However, if you think it is excellent, there is nothing wrong with saying so!

Overall effectiveness: the quality and standards of education

Oddly, overall effectiveness is an easy section to miss when writing your SEF. All your previous information should lead up to making this judgement, so use the evaluation schedule carefully in making your final judgement. Ensure your grades add up: if the quality of education is not good overall, your school cannot be good overall. If it is not outstanding, you cannot be outstanding overall (this is clear in the grade descriptors).

Safeguarding must be 'effective' for your school to be good. Safeguarding is the one limiting judgement for inadequate that survives from the old framework. SMSC and the promotion of pupils' physical well-being can no longer limit your judgement to inadequate, although in practice I would be surprised if they didn't. If one of your other judgements doesn't match your judgement for overall effectiveness, be very clear on why it doesn't. It is possible in 'exceptional circumstances' (grade descriptors, p. 40, S5) for one other judgement to be requires improvement, as long as it is improving rapidly towards good.

Have a read of the grade descriptors for overall effectiveness (p. 40, S5), noting the one descriptor for inadequate. If any one key judgement or safeguarding is judged to be inadequate, you will be inadequate overall.

Finally, good luck. Follow this advice and you will have created a persuasive SEF to show your school in its best light to your inspection team.

SECONDARY SELF-EVALUATION TOOL

How to write your SEF

(Applicable to schools, with or without sixth forms, university technical colleges and studio schools.)

A self-evaluation has only one purpose: to put an idea of the grade you think you deserve in your lead inspector's head. The length of your self-evaluation form (SEF) doesn't matter as much as the telling of a persuasive story.

Don't combine your SEF with your school development plan (SDP). The audience and purpose is very different, and the SDP will hand your lead inspector his or her inspection trails on a plate.

Have the EIF 2019 section 5 handbook with you as you write.

Start your SEF with a clear indication of where you judge your school to be, set out in a separate sentence – for example, 'We believe that X School is a good school.' The rest of your SEF then forms a document to back up that statement. Really, writing an SEF is as easy as that. Then follow the Ofsted handbook areas.

For me, it's about clarity of purpose, and too many schools write an SEF without a clear purpose. In consequence, they include where they are successful but they also expose every weakness under headings such as 'what we need to do to improve'. It can then effectively become a series of inspection trails for your lead inspector and can be evidence that you are not doing things well enough. The SEF should also be written in proud and confident language. It is a document of information but also of persuasion. Wherever you can, illustrate it with positives from your last inspection.

Begin with your school's context, but also make this your Ofsted context, and then include information about your school. You then need a section on information about your school and one on your progress in meeting the issues from your previous inspection, before embarking on an explanation of the main SEF areas.

Context

Context is the second most important section of your SEF after quality of education. This will be the first sight your lead inspector has of your own picture of the school. Briefly detail the intent and implementation of your school's curriculum. Also detail the main points of your published data and how much extra your pupils learn because of the cogency of your curriculum (your impact). State how you believe pupils are progressing in the current school year too. Although the team shouldn't ask for internal tracking data, there is no harm in directing them to the quality of what they will see in class, in books and in talking to all stakeholders, via a statement about how well current pupils are performing across the school (not just in Year 11). Link this to the quality of your curriculum.

In a separate paragraph, describe the level of skills that pupils bring on entry to the school and the progress they make from their starting points. It is so important to establish pupils' skills on entry with a clarity that is persuasive (see more below), so introduce this now. SATs results don't tell the whole story and your pupils may join severely lacking in some areas because of your context. Make sure you give a very clear picture of attainment on entry from primary schools here.

If you re-baseline in any areas, introduce this and expand on it in the impact section, explaining why you feel the need to do so. *Paint this picture as low as you can.* This is one of the most important things you will do in the whole of your SEF. I know Analyse School Performance (ASP) can be difficult to get around but re-baselining can help. This gives the basis for progress across the whole school. Mention the effect of transience, touching on whether any outliers have seriously affected your progress and attainment in ASP. Use proud language throughout. This is your school, so let that show.

A phrase to play about with could be this: 'Our pupils join with skills below those of other pupils nationally and often lower than those indicated in our IDSR. They make progress across the school because of our excellent curriculum provision and good teaching to achieve outcomes approaching national norms on leaving.' In a secondary school facing challenging circumstances, for which GCSE published data can be difficult, this can be an impact lifesaver, if you can persuade your lead inspector that it is true. On inspection, progress begins from pupils' starting points when they joined the school. Your school may do a great job in preparing pupils for the wider world, but your GCSE attainment may not reflect this. Hopefully your progress will, but SATs results can be inflated because of the focus on passing them in Year 6. When they join you, the pupils' knowledge may not have been consolidated and may be lost to their long-term memory.

Use the context statement to bring up the main strengths in an area early, so they are in the mind of the reader before they get to the four (five if you have a sixth form) main inspection areas. Briefly say how the intent behind your curriculum and any recent changes has contributed to improving results. (If not overall improvement, point to particular areas. If improvement is not yet apparent, or you are reorganising your curriculum, explain the intent behind this.) Also mention strengths in safeguarding, governance and spiritual, moral, social and cultural (SMSC) development, so they are also in the mind of your reader before they get to these sections later. If your not in education, employment or training (NEETs) are low, mention this early. It can be a good indicator of an inclusive school that prizes outcomes other than just the academic. It can also be an excellent indicator of how well pupils are prepared for the next stage in their education and helps to fulfil the second bullet under 'impact' in the 'quality of education' grade descriptors (p. 51, S5).

Point the reader in the direction of improvements you have made or are making, especially since the last inspection, and that you have improved considerably since then.

Set out your vision here. Do it succinctly and explain how this is communicated to all staff. If you have a vision statement, make it clear. If you wish to play the game and include curriculum somewhere in that vision, so be it, but all stakeholders need to reflect the school's vision to inspectors, so make the message simple.

Information about this school

The 'information about this school' section from the previous inspection report (updated using the context page in IDSR) will give you much of the other contextual information you need. However, flesh out the deprivation in your catchment with local authority and Income Deprivation Affecting Children Index (IDACI) data.

Progress in meeting the previous Ofsted inspection key issues

Include a separate section on progress to alert your inspectors to the fact that you have addressed these and that progress has been made. Use subheadings for each one.

Main SEF areas

There are five sections in the new inspection framework: quality of education, behaviour and attitudes, personal development, leadership and management, and sixth-form provision. Work using the EIF 2019 section 5 handbook as a guide. The section 8 handbook will inform your inspection if you are a good or outstanding school, but it doesn't include any grade descriptors and you will need these when writing your SEF. You will not be awarded grades, but will instead get an inspection letter from your section 8 inspection team with the three outcomes (para. 72, p. 18, S8). Choose the grade descriptor that reflects your judgement and evidence all the sentences in that judgement grade throughout. Make it clear that there are areas where you feel things are better than in the grade descriptor. Don't flag up areas where you feel progress is not as good (unless you couch the negative in a positive) and don't use language that would direct a lead inspector to an evidence trail that wouldn't be helpful to you.

Organise your self-evaluation to reflect the judgement order of the EIF 2019 handbook. However, although curriculum, via quality of education, has clearly risen up the order of importance, in my opinion your published outcomes will remain a key judgement in the eyes of your lead inspector. My advice here is not to fully believe Ofsted that curriculum will dominate your lead inspector's thinking until this is clearly shown to be the case (although it *may* dominate the on-the-ground inspection techniques and it *may* provide you with an escape route from results that don't look great) and to make the impact of your curriculum on your results thoroughly persuasive, through carefully explaining your pupil outcomes. I will review this advice in a year's time when we have had a chance to fully assess EIF 2019.

Quality of education

Quality of education is by far the most important section for your next inspection. Make no mistake, Ofsted are looking for a particular approach with regard to curriculum intent and implementation – impact remains similar – so organise your SEF accordingly, with three separate subheadings, and play their game. In my opinion, it is too much of a risk, unless your data is stone-cold excellent, to do otherwise, and I truly wish I didn't have to write that. The language you use is important, so I would write your SEF and construct your arguments carefully, reflecting Ofsted's own language at apposite times.

Intent

Make your intent proud and personal and ensure that the strapline, at least, is known by all stakeholders. You have your own context, so the intent of your curriculum may be different to that of other schools (para. 175, p. 42, S5). It should be bespoke to you: what is in your curriculum that is unique to your school? How have you designed your curriculum to reflect this?

The handbook (para. 179, p. 43, S5) says that 'inspectors will draw evidence about leaders' curriculum "intent" principally from discussions with senior and subject leaders', and the bullets in this paragraph give you the specific information to include and explain in your section on curriculum intent. In terms of preparation, there is likely to be a much greater burden on middle leaders in subject deep dives. Ensure they are fully briefed on the school's curriculum intent and how the curriculum intent is then sequenced in their own subject to enhance pupils' knowledge. I fully understand the difficulties of subject leadership in the foundation subjects in primary schools, especially small ones, but this is something that heads are going to have to plan for on inspection. In addition, state that you quality assure your curriculum intent through regular meetings; the need for quality assurance was stressed to inspectors in July 2019 EIF training.

Implementation

Ofsted say (para. 182, p. 44, S5) that 'inspectors will primarily evaluate how the curriculum is taught at subject and classroom level'. The bullets in the succeeding paragraph set out what they will be looking for and therefore what to explain in this section. Ofsted believe that learning can be defined as 'an alteration in long-term memory and not just memorising disconnected facts' (para. 184, p. 45, S5). Show how your improving outcomes are illustrating that this is true, or how your intent and implementation are so well structured that it is clear that pupil outcomes will respond over time. Ofsted assert that they will take account of the fact that curriculum redesign will take time to impact on results, especially in schools in challenging circumstances. (I know – let's hope they actually do!)

I'm sure you have noticed that there is no judgement any more for quality of teaching. Instead, it is in the implementation section where you must link teaching quality to curriculum intent and to impact (results). Look at the grade descriptors at the end of this section under 'implementation' (p. 50, S5). It's all about the work of teachers. Explain how their work leads to your results in this section. Use the grade descriptor bullets to help you (pp. 50–51, S5). It is also worth explaining your reading policy at this stage, together with your phonics planning and provision, and mesh these with your curriculum, as three of the criteria for implementation mention either reading or phonics (the other seven are about teaching).

I will deal with the use of internal assessment data here, but it crops up in both intent and impact. Ofsted are clear that 'Inspectors will not look at non-statutory internal progress and attainment data on section 5 and section 8 inspections of schools' (para. 194, p. 47, S5). However, other paragraphs describe the school's use of assessment, always stepping carefully around their original statement about not asking for data. How inspectors can 'evaluate how assessment is used in the school to support the teaching of the curriculum' (para. 186, p. 45, S5) without looking at current internal data is a mystery. It's a contradiction that, I think, allows you to still use internal assessment data with inspectors, although some will say, 'No, I'm not looking.' Please accept this if they do, but qualify it with something like, 'I'm sure you'll see, in everything we do, that our internal data accurately reflects where we think we are.' Don't let them off the hook if you know your improvement is rapid but is not yet reflected in published results. Direct them to the excellence of your curriculum intent and implementation to support this.

If you feel that your internal assessment procedures give you a good handle on how much progress your pupils are making *and* you can demonstrate accuracy in predictions in previous years, include these data in your SEF, under 'impact', and explain their use, but be mindful of Ofsted's attempts to reduce workload. Be especially mindful of paragraph 189 (p. 45, S5). If Ofsted feel your assessment procedures are work-heavy and your published data is making your lead inspector twitchy, you can bet that he or she will use your assessment procedures as a stick to beat you with, which may result in a letter stating that they will return for a section 5 inspection within one to two years (outcome 3, para. 72, p. 18, S8). If your data is pretty good, the same procedures will probably attract no more than a comment in a 'continuing good' report (outcome 1, para. 72, p. 18, S8). Tread carefully. There is no need to give Ofsted that stick, and unless these issues arise during your inspection you could keep your procedures under the table and deal with them only if that can of worms is opened. Two or three data collection points is what Ofsted are expecting, no more (para. 188, p. 45, S5).

Ofsted describe how they will collect this evidence (para. 189, p. 46, S5), and this can be used in conjunction with, or instead of, internal assessment data to show how you are implementing your curriculum.

Impact

Impact is probably the area of quality of education with which school leaders will be most familiar. It is effectively the old 'pupil outcomes' section of the 2015–2018 framework, combined with how much extra knowledge they have gained. When Ofsted refer to 'what pupils have learned' (para. 192, p. 46, S5), they mean what published results they have gained (or what your internal data is showing, if you can get your inspector to listen).

Ofsted believe that 'all learning builds towards an end point' (para. 193, p. 47, S5) and information sessions about EIF 2019 have indicated that it is up to schools what that end point is. However, the handbook is clear (para. 197, p. 48, S5): GCSE and Year 12/13 examinations are your end points.

Reading progress, and therefore how you integrate and organise the promotion of reading in the curriculum, is especially important to highlight in your SEF. How you evidence progress in reading, especially in Years 7 and 8 for learners who came to you with below age-related expectations for reading, without pointing to internal assessment data is up to you. All stakeholders, especially subject leaders, should be able to talk about how their subject helps pupils to read, and read widely, throughout their time with you.

Structuring impact

Include a short opening context statement in which you state how you can see that pupils' knowledge and skills have moved forward, via your improving strengths in attainment and progress results at GCSE. If these results are not yet there in the inspection year, point again to the excellence of your curriculum intent and implementation and state you are certain this will have a significant future impact.

Repeat the language you have used about skills on entry here and use that to judge progress across the whole school. Try to make progress across all years, and across all subjects and pupil groups at GCSE, as level as possible. If one group is making less than expected progress it can open a huge can of very poisonous worms, so this needs cautious explanation. Explain any possible areas of weakness carefully. There will be a story to tell. Data is key (Ofsted now call data 'performance information' (para. 197, p. 48, S5)). Pack this section full of data and show that you have an excellent grasp of it. Tables are good, but explain each table you include in an accompanying commentary.

Don't be afraid to use other data, over and above your IDSR. Your inspectors will not have seen, say, Fischer Family Trust (FFT) data or progress data from other commercial packages. They will see level 3 data. Use whatever data you can to supplement, or even contradict, the IDSR. Use positive pupil/parent comments and questionnaire data to back up your judgement.

If you have a sixth form, I wouldn't recommend writing about your sixth-form pupils' progress here. The sixth form is not statutory and, apart from safeguarding, will be judged separately.

Possible grade 2 lifelines

- **Transience (stability).** Be very clear on how transience through your school may have affected your GCSE data and also how transience out (easily forgotten) of higher ability pupils has also possibly affected your data (if it has). Next to attainment on entry, high transience can be the key to explaining why progress, and especially attainment, may not be showing correctly in your IDSR. It may just provide you with a lifeline.

- **Outliers.** The effects of outliers, which can be seen in your IDSR scatterplots, can be a possible second grade 2 lifeline. ASP does now exclude the most obvious outliers, but you may have a rash of them in one cohort. I hope your lead inspector understands the effect that outliers – which may lie beyond your control – could have on your progress and attainment data. If they don't, you must tell them! By outliers, I mean the lowest-performing pupils in your IDSR scatterplots.

- **Explain the progress of your current pupils fully.** Even though Ofsted state that inspectors won't consider this data. Data may not be just improving in the current Year 11, but improvements may

173

be clear in other year groups, and progress may already have been accelerating in those year groups during the previous year. If this is the case, your team needs to know this.

Stress these as yet unseen (to your inspectors, through their data) improvements and clearly explain the links to improving curriculum and the quality of leadership and teaching. Tables could be prepared that can be updated easily with your latest data drop straight after the inspection phone call. If you can persuade your inspection team that a corner has already been turned in pupil progress, you may have a vital way into persuading your lead inspector that your school is improving, or that last year's Year 11 data is not the start of a declining trend. On inspection, Ofsted state this will be seen in books, talking to leaders at all levels and especially to pupils about how much extra they know. Thus, Ofsted can leave you alone for at least another three years as a school that continues to be good.

Within your impact data, the progress in English, maths, EBacc and all the various groups need to be covered and outcomes explained: special educational needs and disability (SEND), free school meals, English as an additional language/ethnic minorities, boys/girls, low/medium/ higher attaining pupils. Be especially clear about the progress of disadvantaged pupils, disadvantaged most able pupils and the progress of the most able pupils (a continuing Ofsted focus and mentioned many times in EIF 2019). It is not now whether you are narrowing the gap with non-disadvantaged pupils during their time in your school, but whether you are narrowing the gap with all other pupils nationally. Explain fully why this may not have happened in the past and use current data as well as you can to explain why this is changing. If progress of a particular group appears to be slowing, especially if it is the progress of a disadvantaged group, that can spell trouble; use your current year's data to show the trend is reversing. A picture of a few differences in rates of progress, or even improvements in rates of progress over time, against each group's respective national figures, would be ideal.

Any difficulties or inconsistencies between groups should be explained. If there is standout poor progress of one group, address the reasons with that group's data, and don't forget the importance of data from *current* pupils. It's no use ignoring this if it is clear from your data. Explain it in your SEF in your own terms before you have to do so during an inspection. Don't miss the positives! The 'standout' may be some groups who are doing particularly well!

Don't overlook 'learning well across the curriculum' because here is where you can evidence how you achieve this in numeracy, and especially literacy, by employing other subjects to help. This is likely to be explored in any deep dive into a subject. How individual subjects help all pupils to read widely will be questioned. And don't miss explaining clearly how you ensure your pupils continue to progress in their reading, especially those who came to you with weak skills. Provide data here on the progress of interventions such as reading schemes as evidence that any pupils who may be at risk of falling behind are supported.

Use pupil/parent comments, any outside survey information (e.g. Kirkland Rowell) and questionnaire data to back up your judgement.

Don't forget to look over the grade descriptors (pp. 49–52, S5), checking that you have included information in your 'quality of education' section which would support the bullet points relevant to the grade you want. It is a 'best fit' but that does leave it up to your inspectors and especially your lead inspector. Persuasion is the goal!

Behaviour and attitudes

The first paragraph in this section (para. 201, p. 52, S5) gives you your reason for writing this section. It is about how you create a safe, calm, orderly and positive environment, so that is what you must show. The bullet points in the next paragraph list all the areas you must cover.

Start by judging where you feel behaviour and attitudes is in your school and use the whole section to back up that judgement with quantitative evidence. 'No statement without evidence to back it up' should be your mantra. If you say that continuing professional development has happened, justify with quantitative, monitored evidence that it has had an impact in the classroom. Use specific examples to illustrate and link to outcome data from the 'quality of education' section above.

Paragraphs 205–207 (pp. 53–54, S5) about school culture and sanctions, especially around exclusions (which have risen up the Ofsted agenda), are important. Highlight and explain your procedures and outcomes. Link low exclusions to excellent safeguarding and inclusion. As before, inspectors will choose some SEND case studies to look at, so say that your case studies are robust, secure and helpful to you. Don't miss paragraph 208 (p. 54, S5) on alternative strategies to exclusion: for an inclusive school, this is a good invitation to set out what you do.

Your attendance data over time goes in this section. This needs to show that it is above the lowest 10% nationally and is improving over time. Use whatever you can to evidence this improvement in the current year group. Disaggregate pupils who have left but who are still counting, pupils who are/were on your books for a time but who never arrived, school closures for illness outbreaks, snow days, pupils who have had a severe illness and needed a long time for recovery – whatever you can to show an improvement from the previous year's figures. Few lead inspectors will wish to hang a school on attendance if it is clearly doing well overall. As such, they will value your evidence here to get them out of a potential hole with the HMI who does the quality assurance on their evidence base and report. If attendance is improving, link this to increased engagement through the improving curriculum.

Paragraph 213 and its attendant bullets explain how Ofsted will inspect behaviour and attitudes. Ensure you are fine with these points. There is no need to write about all of them, but elaborate on any issues where the information could be wobbly.

Don't forget to look over the grade descriptors (pp. 57–58, S5), checking that you have included information in your behaviour and attitudes section which would support the bullets relevant to the grade you want. It is a best fit, but that does leave it up to your inspectors and especially your lead inspector. Persuade them!

Personal development

In the EIF, personal development is now separate to behaviour (this used to be 'personal development, behaviour and welfare'). The separation actually gives behaviour and attitudes and personal development a more prominent place in the inspection team's thinking.

Paragraphs 216–217 (p. 58, S5) provide the rationale behind this grade. Intent, implementation and impact are all there, as this is effectively another curriculum section – this time, the wider curriculum (including SMSC) which supports pupils' personal development. It would be well worth organising this section along the lines of the new Ofsted constructs, but it's up to you. Just ensure you mention them, perhaps quite often!

Paragraph 218 (pp. 58–59, S5) outlines all the things you need to evidence in your SEF. Make sure you describe each one, although many could be combined. There is no need for a subheading for each, unless you really wish to do so.

Spiritual, moral, social and cultural development

There are no judgement criteria for SMSC development and it is not judged separately. In many ways, SMSC has been reduced in importance in this framework and inadequate SMSC will no longer lead to grade 4. SMSC has been included in personal development, instead of under overall effectiveness, as it was previously. Still, it is worth giving it its own section.

What is expected of you is clearly set out in paragraphs 219–223 (pp. 59–60, S5), so use subheadings for all four areas and write this according to the bullet points on those pages. There is a great deal of overlap with the promotion of equality of opportunity, the protection of pupils from radicalisation and extremism, and the promotion of traditional British values, which all fall within leadership and management in the handbook. There is nothing wrong with covering all those issues here. It would save duplication.

If your NEETs are below average, particularly if this is combined with low exclusions and no off-rolling, shout this from the rooftops! It can be a strong indicator of an inclusive school and that you are preparing your pupils well for the next phase in their education.

Keep the focus on quantitative evidence and pupil/parent comments – you can use those on Parent View. Any outside survey information (e.g. Kirkland Rowell) or questionnaire data can help here too. In addition, link social and moral education to behaviour and attitudes outcomes wherever you can.

Don't forget to look over the grade descriptors (pp. 62–64, S5), checking that you have included information in your personal development section which would support the bullets relevant to the grade you want. It is a best fit, but that does leave it up to your inspectors and especially your lead inspector. Persuade them!

Leadership and management

Begin by judging the effectiveness of leadership and management in your school and use the whole section to back up that judgement with as much quantitative evidence as you can. Link it especially to pupil outcomes and curriculum improvements. Let your mantra be 'no statement without evidence to back it up' and you won't go far wrong.

Don't be afraid to talk highly of the head teacher here, even if you are writing the section yourself, as the head teacher! You are a crucial part of leadership and management. Use comments from others to do this. Leadership starts with the head teacher or principal, but it needs to be evidenced at all levels.

Paragraph 229 (p. 64, S5) gives you the rationale behind Ofsted's intent – and note their inclusion of the word 'research' in this statement. Play the game in this section and drop in references to the research behind your decisions, especially about curriculum.

The succeeding eight bullets set out the areas you need to write about and evidence.

If you are a part of a multi-academy trust (MAT), the roles and responsibilities of the school within the MAT need to be explained (paras 233–235, p. 65, S5). If you are not, ignore these. This could be done at the start of the next section on governance.

Let each sentence in the handbook's grade descriptors (pp. 74–75, S5) guide you, so you don't leave out things like governors, parents, safeguarding and especially how leaders have conceived and implemented a curriculum bespoke to your school.

There is tangential reference to partnerships in the descriptors, via a mention of trustees if you are in a MAT, but paragraphs 245 and 246 (p. 67, S5) reference partnerships more explicitly, so include it in your writing. If the use of external agencies has been used appropriately and successfully in particular areas (e.g. teaching, behaviour, SMSC), reference this in the individual section, referring to evidence of improvement. Seeking help should not be regarded as weakness; this is about seeking particular expertise that you may not have in the school and can be presented as a positive for leadership and management.

The rest of the leadership and management section is a series of subheadings to evidence the areas to which the handbook gives particular importance. All are included in the inadequate descriptors (p. 75, S5) and are limiting judgements for your grade. That is, fail *any* of these and you will be judged inadequate for leadership and management, and thus grade 4 overall. The following points need to be explained separately:

- Governance.

- Use of the pupil premium and its effectiveness.

- Gaming.

- Inclusion and off-rolling.

- Safeguarding.

Governance

If you are in a MAT, paragraphs 238 and 239 (p. 66, S5) describe how roles and responsibilities should be explained. Don't leave this until the day of inspection for your governors/trustees to explain, although it will be in the lead inspector's checklist to discuss in the 90-minute pre-inspection phone call. Explain your governance structure fully here. If you are not in a MAT, ignore this; your governing body is the responsible body.

Paragraphs 241–243 (pp. 66–67, S5) set out the areas around which Ofsted will ask questions to governors. They stress the importance of the *Governance Handbook* more in this framework,[1] so any inspection governance team must show that they have knowledge of its contents. A knowledge of intent and implementation of the curriculum is also

---

1   Department for Education, *Governance Handbook for Academies, Multi-Academy Trusts and Maintained Schools* (March 2019). Available at: https://www.gov.uk/government/publications/governance-handbook.

necessary. Ensure that your SEF communicates your confidence in your governing body/trustees and that their knowledge is good. If that confidence proves weak, it will leave you vulnerable to requires improvement/ special measures.

A note to your governors here: don't be blindsided by focusing completely on intent and implementation of the curriculum; impact is still important. When asked about this, be prepared to explain the school's results and say how any improvements are related to curriculum and other factors. If improvements are rapid, but are not yet showing fully in published data, don't be afraid to refer to internal data to demonstrate this. Also be prepared to accept an inspector saying that they can't look at it, but counter with, 'Just look at the evidence in classrooms, teaching, books and the ethos and positive learning environment in the school. You can't miss it and we know this through our monitoring.' Something similar could go in the 'quality of education' section of the SEF. Take control, leaders and governors!

Use of the pupil premium

Paragraph 244 (p. 67, S5) outlines your writing points on the pupil premium. Refer to the information on your website for much of this – there is no need to repeat it. Use this section to link your curriculum intent to your rationale for spending the pupil premium and to your results.

Off-site provision

If you use no off-site provision, say so. If you do, paragraphs 247–253 (pp. 67–68, S5) apply. This has been expanded greatly from the previous framework, with inspectors being asked to investigate the use of off-site provision carefully. This is due to Ofsted's focus on unregistered schools, especially those of a religious nature; Ofsted now have a dedicated unregistered schools team. Explain carefully and ensure you know about the registration status of any alternative providers that you use. Paragraph 252 explains the consequences! It is down to you to check, and if Ofsted get a sniff of the use of an unregistered school for alternative provision, the consequence may well be special measures.

Gaming

Gaming is new to this framework and is explained in paragraph 254 (p. 68, S5). It is well worthwhile including a short paragraph explaining why your curriculum and exam entries should not, in any way, come under the label of 'gaming the system'.

Inclusion and off-rolling

Inclusion and off-rolling are also new to this framework. If this doesn't apply to your school, say exactly that. Hopefully, it doesn't apply to you, but if you are off-rolling pupils the consequences are special measures (and should be, in my opinion). Have a read of paragraphs 256–261 (pp. 69–70, S5) and be aware of your responsibilities.

Safeguarding

Safeguarding is a big part of inspection and it is something you simply must get right for your pupils. However, there is a recognition at Ofsted that safeguarding has improved and it may not feel to you that the inspection team's focus is as strong as it used to be. 'Don't open cans of worms' is the overriding maxim here. However, if you have an ongoing safeguarding worry, explain it fully.

Ofsted instruct their inspectors to be familiar with two pieces of statutory guidance in relation to safeguarding, so you should be familiar with them too. I'm sure you know them already. The first is *Keeping Children Safe in Education: Statutory Guidance for Schools and Colleges*[2] and the second is *Working Together to Safeguard Children*.[3] There are also three other 'guides for inspection' listed in the footer on p. 71 (S5) (one is a duplication). These tell inspectors what they must do and how they must do it, so it may be worth knowing their contents.

To go through the intricacies of safeguarding is too big a scope for this SEF tool, or for your SEF, but if you get safeguarding wrong on a daily

---

2   Department for Education, *Keeping Children Safe in Education Statutory Guidance for Schools and Colleges* (September 2019). Available at: https://www.gov.uk/government/publications/keeping-children-safe-in-education--2.

3   Department for Education, *Working Together to Safeguard Children: A Guide to Inter-Agency Working to Safeguard and Promote the Welfare of Children* (July 2018). Available at: https://www.gov.uk/government/publications/working-together-to-safeguard-children--2.

basis, beyond simple administrative errors which can easily be corrected on inspection, you are not doing right by the pupils in your school, and lead inspectors and inspection teams will not be kind. Nor should they be. Write safeguarding as strong, unless it really isn't; but if it isn't, you are very likely to be looking at grade 4 for leadership and management and for overall effectiveness.

It is worth mentioning your website here and whether it is compliant. Your lead inspector has to state whether it is or is not compliant. To do that, of course, you must ensure that it is![4] Follow the link for 'advice on publishing information about your school's governors' because buried in this document is what you should publish on your website regarding governors' interests.[5] If your website is not compliant, because of a particular and valid reason, say so; don't be found out.

In addition, to help your lead inspector, you could add a sentence like this (or copy it, providing it's true): 'There is no negative information, safeguarding or otherwise, of which we are aware, on the Internet or in the local press from the local authority, Department for Education or police concerning our pupils.'

Paragraphs 262–272 (pp. 71–72, S5) give you all the information you need to structure your safeguarding section. Your SCR will be checked. Paragraphs 44 and 53 imply this, although there is no specific mention of it in leadership and management. Make sure that it is up to date, has no gaps (that is what they will scan for) and you can justify the evidence trails that sit behind the content, and say all of this in your SEF.

Evaluating sixth-form provision in schools

This has changed (again) from the previous framework. This section is judged separately, as before. Give one grade overall; there is no need to give grades for each area. However, you may wish to follow the

---

4   All the information that maintained schools should put on their website can be found at: https://www.gov.uk/guidance/what-maintained-schools-must-publish-online.

5   Department for Education, *The Constitution of Governing Bodies of Maintained Schools: Statutory Guidance for Governing Bodies of Maintained Schools and Local Authorities in England* (August 2017), pp. 11–12. Available at: https://www.gov.uk/government/publications/constitution-of-governing-bodies-of-maintained-schools.

requirements of report writing by giving a written grade for each area – for example, 'Leadership and management of the sixth form is outstanding because ...' Your lead inspector will be expected to do this when they write their report. This section could be graded differently to other sections in your SEF, but explain why. The grading of the sixth form will be taken into account, but your lead inspector has the freedom to judge the sixth form differently if they think fit.

Notice that it is no longer 16–19 study programmes, but is back to sixth-form provision, so make sure you change your subheading when updating your SEF.

Organise your sixth-form section into the following areas:

▪ Context.

▪ Quality of education.

▪ Behaviour and attitudes.

▪ Personal development.

▪ Leadership and management.

The bullets in paragraph 292 (p. 83, S5) give you the areas on which to focus in your writing, but I would use the structure above to organise this section.

Context

Set out the context of your sixth form in a short statement. State how many progress to your sixth form or join from other schools. Give the attainment on entry to your sixth form and highlight any difficulties this may pose, if it is below average. Describe expectations and ethos in the sixth form.

Quality of education in the sixth form

Within quality of education, curriculum intent and implementation are important, but I believe that the impact of sixth-form provision will still have a pull on your inspectors' minds, so explain this well.

I would recommend explaining your outcomes here, rather than in your main 'quality of education' section, as this is a separate, non-statutory part of the school and, usually, new pupils have joined from elsewhere. Use your level 3 value-added report alongside other reports such as FFT.

Paragraph 293 (p. 83, S5) and the subsequent grade descriptors will help you to include what is relevant to inspectors. The grade descriptors for 'evaluating sixth-form provision' are not organised under intent, implementation and impact, but intent is mentioned in the grade descriptors here: 'Staff create the intent of an ambitious, coherently planned and sequenced curriculum.' I'd approach this section with the three sub-headings of intent, implementation and impact to reflect the knowledge that the school has about this framework and that all staff are aware. Structure it in a similar way to your main school 'quality of education' section.

Paragraph 292 (second bullet, p. 83, S5) reminds you that inspectors will look closely at the curriculum you provide for learners without GCSE grades 9 to 4. Describe work experience here.

Ofsted have got the traditional, knowledge-based curriculum bit between their teeth in this framework and it shows through in the grade descriptors for evaluating sixth-form provision. They also expect to see a curriculum bespoke to your setting and context. Progress is the key. If you can persuade them that your students make good progress, they are more likely to say that your curriculum supports this than if they feel progress is weak.

Behaviour and attitudes in the sixth form

Apply similar writing criteria to the main behaviour and attitudes section, but this doesn't have to be a long section. Be positive about how well your sixth formers settle in and, hopefully, inspectors will see that. Mention their attendance and the numbers progressing to Year 13.

Talk about the low numbers (if they are) of students that go NEET after the sixth form and the quality of destinations (important especially for pupil referral units and university technical colleges).

Reference the quality of your careers guidance under a subheading here (para. 292, p. 83, S5).

Personal development in the sixth form

Students' personal, social and independent learning skills are explicitly referenced in the first bullet point of paragraph 293 (p. 83, S5). It's worth using this as a basis for writing this section. In addition, mirror what you have written in your main 'personal development' section.

Leadership and management in the sixth form

Link the effectiveness of leadership and management in the sixth form to your outcomes and especially to progress. Explain how leaders have carefully designed a curriculum to focus on the needs of your students and on progression through the study programmes. Show how you use assessment well and how you create an environment that allows sixth formers to focus on learning (both appear in the grade descriptors).

Familiarise yourself with the grade descriptors at the end of the section (pp. 83–86, S5). These will help you to cover all areas around which you will be inspected.

Paragraph 291 (p. 83, S5) makes it clear that the effectiveness of the arrangements for safeguarding students in the sixth form is reflected in the main judgement for the school. However, if you think it is excellent, there is nothing wrong with saying so!

Overall effectiveness: the quality and standards of education

Oddly, overall effectiveness is an easy section to miss when writing your SEF. All your previous information should lead up to making this judgement, so use the evaluation schedule carefully in making your final judgement. Ensure your grades add up: if the quality of education is not good overall, your school cannot be good overall. If it is not outstanding, you cannot be outstanding overall (this is clear in the grade descriptors).

Safeguarding must be 'effective' for your school to be good. Safeguarding is the one limiting judgement for inadequate that survives from the old framework. SMSC and the promotion of students' physical well-being can no longer limit your judgement to inadequate, although in practice I would be surprised if they didn't. If one of your other judgements doesn't match your judgement for overall effectiveness, be very clear on why it doesn't. It is possible in 'exceptional circumstances' (grade descriptors, p. 50, S5) for one other judgement to be requires improvement, as long as it is improving rapidly towards good.

Have a read of the grade descriptors for overall effectiveness (p. 40, S5), noting the one descriptor for inadequate. If any one key judgement or safeguarding is judged to be inadequate, you will be inadequate overall.

Finally, good luck. Follow this advice and you will have created a persuasive SEF to show your school in its best light to your inspection team.

REFERENCES

Allen-Kinross, Pippa (2019) New inspections 'still disadvantage' less affluent schools, analysis suggests, *Schools Week* (2 November). Available at: https://schoolsweek.co.uk/new-inspections-still-disadvantage-less-affluent-schools-analysis-suggests.

Department for Education (2017) *The Constitution of Governing Bodies of Maintained Schools: Statutory Guidance for Governing Bodies of Maintained Schools and Local Authorities in England* (August). Available at: https://www.gov.uk/government/publications/constitution-of-governing-bodies-of-maintained-schools.

Department for Education (2018) *Working Together to Safeguard Children: A Guide to Inter-Agency Working to Safeguard and Promote the Welfare of Children* (July). Available at: https://www.gov.uk/government/publications/working-together-to-safeguard-children--2.

Department for Education (2019a) *Governance Handbook for Academies, Multi-Academy Trusts and Maintained Schools* (March). Available at: https://www.gov.uk/government/publications/governance-handbook.

Department for Education (2019b) *Keeping Children Safe in Education: Statutory Guidance for Schools and Colleges* (September). Available at: https://www.gov.uk/government/publications/keeping-children-safe-in-education--2.

Department for Education (2019c) *Primary School Accountability in 2019: A Technical Guide for Primary Maintained Schools, Academies and Free Schools* (December). Available at: https://www.gov.uk/government/publications/primary-school-accountability.

Department for Education (2019d) *Secondary Accountability Measures: Guide for Maintained Secondary Schools, Academies and Free Schools* (October). Available at: https://www.gov.uk/government/publications/progress-8-school-performance-measure.

Fearn, Heather (2019) Busting the 'intent' myth, *Ofsted Blog: Schools, Early Years, Further Education and Skills* (1 July). Available

at: https://educationinspection.blog.gov.uk/2019/07/01/
busting-the-intent-myth.

Garvey, Paul (2017a) *Taking Control: How to Prepare for Inspection*
(Woodbridge: John Catt).

Garvey, Paul (2017b) *Talk for Teaching: Rethinking Professional
Development in Schools* (Woodbridge: John Catt).

Headteachers' Roundtable (2016) *The Alternative Green Paper:
Schools That Enable All to Thrive and Flourish* (London: Schools
Week). Available at: https://headteachersroundtable.files.wordpress.
com/2016/09/htrt-the-alternative-green-paper-schools-that-enable-
all-to-thrive-and-flourish.pdf.

Morris, Estelle (2011) Exempting schools from Ofsted inspection is a
worrying policy, *The Guardian* (21 November). Available at:
https://www.theguardian.com/education/2011/nov/21/ofsted-
inspections-outstanding-schools-exempt.

Mulholland, Helene (2019) Ofsted amends 'inadequate' grade after
curriculum inspection complaints, *Schools Week* (31 January). Available
at: https://schoolsweek.co.uk/ofsted-amends-inadequate-grade-after-
curriculum-inspection-complaints/.

Office of the Press Secretary (2006) President Bush Addresses
NAACP Annual Convention, Washington (20 July). Available
at: https://georgewbush-whitehouse.archives.gov/news/
releases/2006/07/20060720.html.

Ofsted (2014) *Raising Standards, Improving Lives: The Office for
Standards in Education, Children's Services and Skills (Ofsted) Strategic
Plan 2014 to 2016.* Ref: 140128. Available at: https://www.gov.uk/
government/publications/raising-standards-improving-lives-ofsted-
strategic-plan-2014-to-2016.

Ofsted (2015) *The Future of Education: Understanding the Changes*
(June). Available at: https://www.gov.uk/guidance/changes-to-
education-inspection-from-september-2015.

Ofsted (2018a) *School Inspection Handbook – Section 5* [withdrawn].
Ref: 150066. Available at: https://www.gov.uk/government/
publications/school-inspection-handbook-from-september-2015.

Ofsted (2018b) *School Inspection Handbook – Section 8* [withdrawn].
Ref: 150077. Available at: https://www.gov.uk/government/

publications/handbook-for-short-monitoring-and-unannounced-behaviour-school-inspections.

Ofsted (2019a) *Annual Report and Accounts 2018–19*. HC 2398. Available at: https://www.gov.uk/government/publications/ofsted-annual-report-and-accounts.

Ofsted (2019b) *Education Inspection Framework*. Ref: 190015. Available at: https://www.gov.uk/government/publications/education-inspection-framework.

Ofsted (2019c) *Inspecting the Curriculum: Revising Inspection Methodology to Support the Education Inspection Framework*. Ref: 190024. Available at: https://www.gov.uk/government/publications/inspecting-the-curriculum.

Ofsted (2019d) *School Inspection Handbook – Section 5*. Ref: 190017. Available at: https://www.gov.uk/government/publications/school-inspection-handbook-eif.

Ofsted (2019e) *School Inspection Handbook – Section 8*. Ref: 190019. Available at: https://www.gov.uk/government/publications/section-8-school-inspection-handbook-eif.

Rumsfeld, Donald H. (2002) Department of Defense news briefing (12 February). Available at: https://archive.defense.gov/Transcripts/Transcript.aspx?TranscriptID=2636.

Select Committee on Education (2017) *Multi-Academy Trusts*, 27 February, HC 204 2016–17. Available at: https://publications.parliament.uk/pa/cm201617/cmselect/cmeduc/204/20403.htm.

Wainwright, Daniel (2019) Ofsted: 1,010 'outstanding' schools not inspected for a decade, *BBC News* (2 October). Available at: https://www.bbc.co.uk/news/uk-england-49579520.

Whittaker, Freddie (2019) Ministers have U-turned on 33 attempts to force schools to become academies, *Schools Week* (5 April). Available at: https://schoolsweek.co.uk/ministers-have-u-turned-on-33-attempts-to-force-schools-to-become-academies.

When the Adults Change, Everything Changes

Seismic Shifts in School Behaviour

Paul Dix

ISBN: 978-178135273-1

Drawing on anecdotal case studies, scripted interventions and approaches which have been tried and tested in a range of contexts, from the most challenging urban comprehensives to the most privileged international schools, behaviour training expert Paul Dix advocates an inclusive approach that is practical, transformative and rippling with respect for staff and learners. An approach in which behavioural expectations and boundaries are exemplified by people, not by a thousand rules that nobody can recall.

When the Adults Change, Everything Changes illustrates how, with their traditional sanction- and exclusion-led methods, the 'punishment brigade' are losing the argument. It outlines how each school can build authentic practice on a stable platform, resulting in shifts in daily rules and routines, in how we deal with the angriest learners, in restorative practice and in how we appreciate positive behaviour.

Each chapter is themed and concludes with three helpful checklists – Testing, Watch out for and Nuggets – designed to help you form your own behaviour blueprint. Throughout the book both class teachers and school leaders will find indispensable advice about how to involve all staff in developing a whole-school ethos built on kindness, empathy and understanding.

Suitable for all head teachers, school leaders, teachers, NQTs and classroom assistants – in any phase or context, including SEND and alternative provision settings – who are looking to upgrade their own classroom management or school behaviour plan.

 Also available from www.crownhouse.co.uk: *When the Adults Change, Everything Changes Audiobook* (Abridged Version) ISBN 978-178135314-1